WORKPLACE VOODOO

Denise N.A. Bacchus, PhD

CONTENTS i

DEDICATION

THIS BOOK IS DEDICATED TO
THE UNFUCKWITHABLE
GODDESS
WITHIN
YOU.

ACKNOWLEDGMENT

To God,
Goddess,
I AM
and everyone
who supported
me in the
production
of this book.

FOREWARD

Dr. Denise Bacchus is a rare woman of beauty and power. When I first met her, my initial thought was, *now there's one of the most powerful women I've ever met*. Since then, she's proven it. Power, strength, beauty and wits, all rolled into one. This book is a reflection of the strength and grace she exudes. There are many women who are powerful, yet I've found there are fewer women who are willing to OWN, EMBRACE and CHANNEL this power for GOOD of self and all.

As a beloved member of our global spiritual community, Dr. Denise travels the world with us as The Beautiful Witch Doctor, teacher, and light for all who would follow.

I love hearing about the retreat center she's creating, and the women she's here to support in releasing stress; especially workplace stress, and especially women of color, by spiritual means. 'Dr. B on the Beach' is a clarion call to all women who are drawing identity from a power suit to ditch it for a bathing suit. That's exactly what Dr. Denise did. She traded being suited up, as a stressed-out Professor, to being prayed up, as a blissful reality creator, who just happens to love to wear bathing suits. May this, her first book (and I pray she writes many more), be received with the greatest of welcomes from women all over the world who require a solution to one of our deadliest plagues: stress.

If you're reading this and wondering if you should buy this book, do not hesitate. Buy it now. It holds the answers to workplace stress with spiritual protocols that are shared here like recipes for your freedom. You want to be stress-free, to experience and express the luscious life you were born for. Let this be the solution you're seeking.

You are loved,

Rev. Valerie Love (aka KAISI)

If you take 100% responsibility for your choices,
you cannot be a victim. Rev. Valerie Love

THE WARNING

This book is NOT for the hyper-religious or the hyper-spiritual. Religious or spiritual beliefs are NOT up for debate or question, rather reflection…If the reader chooses
   1. to do so.

   2. This book invites the reader to be open and expand consciousness. If this is agreeable, continue reading.

   3. The title of this book is <u>supposed to be provocative.</u> The title stirs up interest, is tantalizing, alluring, and, most importantly, move one to purchase. How else would this information circulate if no one purchased this book? I wish all purchasers a billion-fold return of prosperity for sowing into this book!

   4. A book entitled <u>Workplace Voodoo</u> should make one wonder if this stuff is going on at the job, and if so, who is doing it? Precisely what are they doing, and how?

   5. There are two biases found in this book. First, the book has a strong lean toward the Judeo-Christian religion and belief system. The majority of the respondents in the study were members of one of the many Christian denominations.

Second, the Bible was used throughout the book as a reference to support spiritual principles.

6. Data for this book came from two scientific studies with college-educated women.

7. The term *professional Black woman* is used to describe Black women who have achieved post-secondary education and beyond as well as employment in white-collar professional occupations.

THE INTENTION

The intention of this book is ELEVATION. This book intends to reveal delicious information about ***how*** spirituality is used as a resource for coping with work-related stress. This book describes ***how*** Black women authentically and naturally express their spirituality and connection to God, Source, or the Higher Intelligence that governs all things in the Universe. It addresses ***how*** to elevate consciousness and end work-related stress. This book helps the seeker acknowledge their divinity and teach them ***how*** to align with their life's divine plan.

WHO IS THIS BOOK FOR

1. This book is for women who are wondering how long they are going to suffer in a job that does not honor them or their talents and skills.

2. This book is for women who are looking to understand themselves and their circumstances at a deeper spiritual level. They want to know they are on the right path.

3. This book is for women who know what they are doing right now for employment might not be what they are supposed to be doing with their lives.

4. This book is for women who genuinely want to be free but may not know the next steps.

5. This book is for women who wonder why negative things happen to them on the job.

6. The book is for women who are continually trying to connect the dots. How do the events of my life fit together?

7. This book is for women who quit their jobs or got fired. They are scared, probably terrified, yet they know there is no going back to a J.O.B. that almost killed them.

THE PURPOSE

The purpose of this book is not to answer existential questions, but to question answers. Does one ever question what they are doing with their life? Are they a doctor because God sent them to Earth to become doctors, or did they decide to become doctors based on fulfilling an *egoic* need to feel special? Are they working for money? The recognition? Respect? The authority? The necessity?

Problems on the job are a significant way for God to get one's attention. Many will not utter a prayer or fall to their knees in supplication until they experience hell. It is then they begin praying, call friends, reach out to the pastor or elders, or do something proactive about the situation. So, we count it all joy when suffering. Job stress may bring us to a face-to-face encounter with our *higher Self* and God.

Job stress signals one has strayed from the "God plan" for their life. Workplace Voodoo is a mechanism to recalibrate them back on the path to God. If they intuitively knew they did not come to Earth to be a slave, Workplace Voodoo is for them.

Read this book. Learn what other women like these are doing to transform the work atmosphere from negative to positive. Learn how these professional Black women learned to raise their level of consciousness so they would never experience work-related stress. Furthermore, if they did, they would know what to do about it. Believe it or not, their co-workers already know. Besides, some are already doing it!

GALACTIC SIGNATURE

White Electric Mirror

I am a unique divine soul.

My Divine Purpose is to see myself as I am, shadow included, freed from the maze of mental illusion.

Join me on my spiritual journey where there is no good or bad, no right or wrong —there is only the reflection of what is.

I am open and willing to examine the information I see in my mirrors and use it to transform inherited dysfunctional belief systems, negative thought forms, and fixed patterns.

As I learn to see myself, I begin to see my emotional reactions as signs indicating where to focus my awareness for growth.

The greatest gift I have uncovered is the power of forgiveness.

Forgiveness is a decision.

My freedom emerged from forgiveness.

Forgiveness releases me from everything I may judge or see as imperfect and releases me from the perils of the Law of Cause and Effect.

I am White Mirror.

*I am able to clearly reflect **you** back to **yourself**.*

The Truth is a Beautiful Gift.

Dr. B

*"When pain, misery, or anger happen, it is time to look within you,
not around you."*
—*Sadhguru*

All is Conscious. All is GOD.
I AM sustained and cared for by the power of God deep within me.
—FireFairy Wytch

⌘

If you cannot find your passion, you will find a job.
—*Ralph Smart*

1 CHAPTER 1

INTRODUCTION

The stress occurs because the story is not true. We created a story about our existence and found a job to reflect this belief. Many women so strongly identify with their role as workers that they believe God called them to punch a clock, push paper, write reports, or crank out widgets. Some are willing to argue that they know without a shadow of doubt they are here to perform some government job or hold some executive position in the most marginalized department of someone's Fortune 400 corporation. Some have gotten angry and highly defensive at the suggestion there may be another truth. They believe God blessed them with that job, and they are grateful. They love their office, the parking space, the upgraded kitchen snacks, and all the other perks of their excellent corporate job. We get it. They are grateful for the opportunity to work and pay bills. Many that have crossed my path hold similar thoughts and beliefs. I once believed this too.

I did all of those things myself. I enjoyed the fruit of my labor. I took care of my family. I tithed. I traveled. I shopped. Life was great. Yet, I always knew there was something about me that did not align with the model of going to college, getting a job, working hard for 30-40 years, retirement, and dying. There had to be more to life than slaving in the rat race. I had to find out the truth.

I know now most jobs are a major distraction along the path to your divine purpose. They usually take you away from the very thing you love doing the most—expressing your divine self.

Some jobs do allow you to express your divine self. There is the example of the woman who cleans houses. She knows this is her divine calling because she says she is not just cleaning houses; she is bringing order to her clients' lives. This represents spiritual alignment with her occupation because *order* is the first law of the Universe. Most jobs are designed to suppress your authentic creative energy. They really are. I meet people who are poets, painters, artists, singers, or dancers masquerading in life as social workers, lawyers, doctors, or the Vice President of such and such, etc.

The truth is employers pay workers to do what they say, not to create. They are not looking for you to engage in creative self-expression. Do you think you got the job based on your qualifications or skills? Really?? It is more likely you got the job because the employer profiled you as the type who would not challenge the status quo. They use coded language like,

We think this candidate is a good fit for the company.

Employers are looking for the *"good boy"* or *"good girl"* who will religiously come to work and do as they are told. If you are rough around the edges, they have methods to help you conform to maintain the status quo. They pay you just enough so you will not quit and trick you with inducements to keep you happy and make you feel special. These inducements are things like plastic plaques made in China inscribed with *"Employee of the Month."* It is incredible how employees will compete to win a paper certificate or a $25.00

gift card for good behavior. You see this as evidence your employer cares about you. In reality, the employer cares about achieving *its* mission, not your vision.

In the case of professional Black women (PBW), work has been an essential and all-encompassing aspect of their lives. Let's reflect for a moment. From the time they arrived on the shores in 1619 (or earlier depending on which book you read), African women were enslaved on plantations, working from *"can't see in the morning to can't see at night."*

Four hundred plus years of physical and mental enslavement says not only did these women cope with work-related stress—they survived it. Black women's presence in the diaspora is documentation of their survival. Enslaved Black women were deeply spiritual people who knew how to tap into their spirituality as a resource for coping with the atrocities of plantation life. Modern-day Black women have the same power, yet they choose career paths that expose them to the tripartite stress of being Black, female, and undervalued on modern public and/or private corporate plantations.

This book taps into the **HOW**. How do professional Black women use their spirituality as a resource for coping with work-related stress? A sample (n= 203) professional Black women answered a questionnaire about their experiences with work-related stress and the ways they coped with it. In-depth interviews were conducted with ten (N=10) women from the original study to gain a better understanding of their definition of spirituality and how it operates to reduce or eliminate work-related stress.

Black women are entering the professional workforce at a higher rate than ever. Today almost all Black women have to work. The concept of the stay at home mom is a fantasy for many and impossibility for most. Female-headed households are increasing, thereby increasing the number of women who voluntarily enter the workforce and those who are forced to work out of economic necessity. The workplace is where women spend large chunks of their day and many bring their work home. So many women are intimately identified with their role as workers; they totally dissociate with the idea their lives have a divine purpose. They have traded the God Plan for their life for the plan they created for themselves. Although the Bible clearly states,

> *For I know the plans I have for you, declares the LORD, plans to prosper you and not to harm you, plans to give you hope and a future (Jeremiah 29:11).*

Why are women stressed out on the job? According to my research, women are stressed out on the job because they have a job (Bacchus, 2002). That is the short answer. Punching a clock or worse yet, being on salary was never God's plan for your life. The long answer has to do with social positioning and the historical context of when and where Black women entered the United States. Being female and of color automatically means there are ample opportunities to encounter job stress or stressful situations related to race, ethnicity, gender, and age-based prejudice, and discrimination. That is one way of looking at it. Another way is to consider whether the experience of job stress is calling for you to pay attention to what you are doing with your life. Are you willing to cope, or are you ready to exit this painful illusionary matrix?

WHY I WROTE THIS BOOK

I wrote this book for both you and me. Why? Because now is the right time for me to share my research findings and experiences with work-related stress in a nonscientific book. I do so with the hope this book will help you understand the dynamics of this thing we call life, and the role jobs play on the path to our true purpose. I wrote this book because I wished there was a book like this available to me when I was going through hell on the job. I needed to read something that would give me some insight into what I was experiencing and why. Although I read widely both academically and non-academically, I could not find one book that dug deep enough into the root causes of work-related stress or offered an appropriate intervention that would work for women like me.

Who are women like me? Women like me believe we must work hard to achieve anything worthwhile in life. We have spent many years complicating our lives earning degrees, accumulating debt, and competing for high-ranking positions in academic or corporate America. Women like me are the primary caretakers of our immediate family and frequently the extended family. Women like me have multiple competing roles, we believe we must fulfill and function well in and at a high level, in every capacity or else. We hold memberships in several public service or charitable organizations that demand our precious time and energy. We do so to satisfy our need to give back to the *"deserving less fortunate."* We have been infected with the program that we must *"lift as we climb,"* or we are seen as a betrayal to the entire race. Women like me are highly educated, high achieving, and highly stressed out on the job. Yet, we cannot articulate a sound reason (other than money) why we believe we must continue to do what we are doing—slowly killing ourselves. Women like me are often entangled in workplace drama. We are often targets for harassment. We may not even be aware we are targets. Women like me are hardworking and try to rise above the work environment's pettiness, yet we seemed to attract foolishness all the time.

I was continually attracting negativity in almost every work environment I entered, and I could never figure out why. *Why me?* I always performed well. I was highly qualified, yet I continued to attract the attention of bullies and backstabbers.

I wrote this book because <u>Workplace Voodoo</u> reveals secrets, rituals, and practices professional Black women reported using to end work-related stress. I wrote this book because I studied coping with work-related stress for almost 20 years, and I know work-related stress is never going away. If you intend to be successful in the workplace, it is best to be fully equipped on every level-body, mind, soul, and spirit. Read this book from cover to cover. You cannot afford to wait another second.

*I am the wisest man alive, for I know one thing, and that is that
I know nothing.* — *Plato, The Republic*

2 CHAPTER 2

THE KNOWN

Your existence in this incarnation is evidence you are repeating a story. What story? Where did this story come from? If you dare to find out, continue reading. If you think you are merely a body, you are not. You are a combination of a body, a soul, a divine spirit, and the ego. It is easy to recognize the body. It is your physical form or the physical expression of God's creation. You can see, touch, and experience the physical world with the body. It is the learning device of your subconscious mind. Your soul is internal. It is the part of you that leads you on a fantastic journey called your life. Your spirit is the essence of God. It is the part of you that reminds you of your divinity; it is your *higher Self.* The miracle of breath in your lungs is the evidence of God Spirit, the proof of your divinity. Your ego is the fearful part of your mind that created the illusionary world of your thought life, expressed as the life you are living. This life may be in direct opposition to the divine blueprint God created for you.

Your ego has tricked you into believing you are everything, but divine. It has built a case with supporting evidence that you are just a body, separate from the Source that created you. The truth is, you did not create yourself. So, you do not know the purpose of your life. Only the Creator knows the purpose of the things It establishes; therefore, only the Creator of you knows the purpose for your life.

However, your ego has a plan. A plan it made up and is executing in your current consciousness. Why? Because you believe the ego is the real you. You cannot get rid of the ego because you empower it daily with your thoughts. Since the ego does not represent the real you, the story it created, (e.g. doctor, lawyer, engineer, politician, social worker, coach, teacher, CEO, etc.) is not your true reality.

The Study

I conducted this scientific study because I wanted to know how college-educated Black women coped with work-related stress (Bacchus, 2002). Before beginning my research, I asked college educated women around me how they coped with work-related stress. No one could offer me a definite answer or one that made sense. Most of them said they did not know. They did not know *how* they managed all aspects of their lives and still showed up for work and were productive.

I reflected on my own experiences. I was fortunate to be raised by an educated mother. She attended nursing school in Guyana, South America and was a registered nurse before I was born. She immigrated to the United States and worked around the clock to support herself and to send a remittance to my grandmother for our care. When the family reunited in the United States, she was married with three school-aged children. A few years later she was divorced with four children and a house to maintain by herself. The child support was lean. Instead of working things out with my father, I witnessed her scurrying around in what seemed like a never-ending cycle from job to job, dropping us off and picking us up from school, getting very little sleep and repeating this schedule day in and day out. She was exhausted, yet still carved out time to maintain a home, take care of her aging parents, and operate her side hustles to bring in extra cash. Her schedule was simply daunting; she, or her ego had convinced mind this was the only way to live.

While taking on my challenge of graduate school, I was also a single mother, a full-time doctoral student, and a full-time employee. I had my side hustle, a consulting business that entailed frequent out of town travel. I had church obligations. I attended numerous extracurricular activities for my young daughter. I was a homeowner, which meant I had to manage the upkeep and maintenance of the home as well as having time for myself and other personal and family obligations.

One day I looked up and realized I was replicating my mother's life story to spec! By the time my mother was in her mid 40's, she was dealing with a list of health problems, most of them stress-exasperating illnesses and carried around a bag of prescription medicines. I was on the cusp of graduating with the highest degree in academe and I too was diagnosed with a major stress-exacerbating illness and began to carry around a bag of prescription medicines. I was horrified! I saw my future and myself in my mother's experience. I also saw this pattern in the experiences of the many highly educated Black women around me.

On the surface, these women were truly inspirational. Many of them were the first in their families to attend college and they were experiencing great success in their professional appointments. However, they were working themselves into an early grave. Most were chronically ill, overweight, and stressed out. Yet, they still went to work.

How were they doing this? I had to know. I wanted a way out of this madness, so I chose to study it. I dedicated my doctoral research to understand *how* women coped with everything on their plate. I knew if I could find the answer, it would help me and numerous women like myself who were on track for obtaining high-ranking positions in their chosen career path.

Figure 1: Coping Conceptual Model

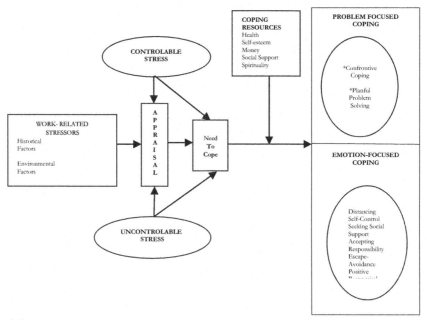

Theoretical Assumption

Descriptive empirical studies about this topic were sparse at best, so I had to begin at the theoretical level. My dissertation committee Chair suggested I apply Lazarus and Folkman's

(1982) model of coping to Black women's case to get a conceptual understanding of the path from stress appraisal to coping outcome. Lazarus and Folkman's coping framework (see Figure 1) posits that stress is ubiquitous and exists externally. They suggest all humans are vulnerable to environmental stressors; however, one's cognitive appraisal of each stressor acts as a filter or buffer for the experience of stress. Therefore, as you encounter a stressor, your cognitive faculties determine whether you appraise the stressor as benign or capable of causing harm, threat, or loss. This model also includes an appraisal of perceived control— do you have a sense you have psychological control to overcome the effect of the stressor given the resources you have for coping? If you decide you have some measure of control over the stressor and adequate support for coping, you will choose to cope. This coping looks like a decision to continue working for an unreasonable boss or remaining in a job that is slowly killing you.

As the theory follows, there are two possible coping outcomes—*emotion-focused coping* (EFC) and *problem-focused coping* (PFC). EFC involves regulating your emotions or doing something to feel better in response to the upset arising from the stressor. EFC activities ranged from seeking social support, comfort, change of scenery, and distraction to denial, using food, sex, alcohol, recreational and/or prescription drugs, and other destructive behaviors to cope. Conversely, PFC entails doing something directly to address the source of the stress. So, if your boss is the issue, PFC says you would use the chain of command to approach the boss and deal with the issue directly. PFC is the preferred and psychologically healthier coping approach because, as the theory presumes, the aim of PFC is problem-resolution. Given this theory, which was never developed with the understanding of the intersection of race, gender, and social positioning as it applies to Black women, issues of power and power relationships on the job influence the likelihood Black women would use PFC in response to work-related stress.

The Results

After applying rigorous research methods and crunching the numbers, study results indicated Black women's way of coping with work-related stress does not align with Lazarus and Folkman's (1982) theory. As expected, PBW who scored high on the stress variable, expressed a lower perception of personal power or *locus of control* over work-related stressors engaged in were more likely to report EFC. Therefore, it was expected to see EFC reported more frequently as the coping outcome among those feeling *less control* (e.g., more powerlessness) over their situation on the job.

A second fantastic finding was PBW who indicated they were *more spiritual* and perceived *more control* over the stressor reported **less** work-related stress. This can be interpreted as a PBW who considers themselves more spiritual are less likely to experience the adverse effects of work-related stress. Furthermore, study participants reported "*spirituality*" as the most frequently used resource for coping with work-related stress. The story could have ended there; however, I did not know *how* these women were defining *spirituality*. Also, I had insufficient data to describe *how* they were using *spirituality* to cope with work-related stress. I wanted to know *how* they defined spirituality and *how* it was used as a buffer for the experience of work-related stress (Bacchus, 2008; Bell, Rajenan, and Theiler, 2012). These findings were the impetus for further inquiry.

So, I asked:

> *How do you engage your spirituality to cope with work-related stress?*
> *What exactly do you do? How does your spirituality operate?*
> *Is spirituality practical for reducing or ending the negative the outcome of work-related stress?*

The Follow Up

In 2003, I conducted a follow up qualitative study with 10 (N=10) women from the original quantitative survey to gain answers to these questions. These interviews uncovered a major methodological flaw in the dependent measure, *Ways of Coping* (Folkman, Lazarus, Gruen, and DeLongis, 1986). Because prayer and spirituality were included on the EFC scale and not on the PFC scale, it appeared women who reported *use of spirituality* as a way of coping with work-related stress preferred EFC to PFC.

However, qualitative analysis revealed PBW believed that when they prayed and/or tapped into their spirituality, they were doing something directly to address the source of stress. When they prayed or meditated about the stressor, they did not avoid the stress; instead, they were doing something directly to address the source of the stress and they expected positive results. Thus, for Black women, spiritual coping *is* problem-focused coping and not emotion-focused coping. Until this study, a result like this has not been documented in empirical studies.

Spirituality Defined

Results from the follow-up study defined spirituality in this context and produced a *3-Factor* **religiosity-spirituality model**.

1. **No Difference**: religion and spirituality are the same.

> *"There is no difference between my religion and my spiritual beliefs."*

2. **A Continuum**: Religious/spiritual beliefs on a continuum from:

> *"My spirituality is rooted in my religious beliefs" to "I am more spiritual than religious."*

3. **Totally Separate**: Spirituality is totally separate and distinct from any religion or religious belief.

> *"My spirituality has nothing to do with religion."*
> *"It is not connected to an organized religion or its dogma."*

Women in Category 3 strongly expressed they are not religious, but spiritual. I interpreted these findings to mean some women see religion and spirituality as the same. In contrast, some see religion and spirituality on a continuum or polarity from *highly religious* to *highly spiritual*. A smaller subset of these women sees their spirituality as being totally separate from religion.

I was amazed at these responses. So, I dug deeper. Study subjects reported engaging in religious activities like fasting and praying to engaging in traditional African spiritual practices involving ancestors and deity worship. Some reported performing magick spells! Now had a better understanding of the previous finding indicating PBW who reported *lower stress,* were more likely to report Category 3— *"my spirituality is totally separate from any religious beliefs."*

Spirituality as a Resource for Coping

This smaller group of PBW, who considered themselves spiritual and not religious, engaged in activities found outside of traditional religious doctrine. They used their connection sources to provide answers for the experience of stress. They used this insight not just to cope but overcome work-related stress. The Bible scripture below supports this course of action,

Be still, and know that I am God (Psalm 46:10).

This finding is huge simply because science does not understand how spirituality operates. Scientists have been reluctant to explore spirituality in empirical studies claiming it is not scientifically observable; therefore, it is not scientifically knowable. Scientists focused on discernible cause and effect—detecting associations between independent and dependent variables and describing their acceptable statistical significance level. Study subjects explained their understanding of stress based on their knowledge of the Universal Law of cause and effect. They felt religion was useful in providing holy books, a doctrine, a code of behavior, a guide for sacred practices, a house of worship, stories, a concept of heaven and hell, and punishment for sin. Spirituality, on the other hand, has everything to do with letting go of religious programming and becoming more connected to the Divine (e.g., Source,

God, Jehovah, Allah, etc.), to nature, and the Source of everything. These women identified themselves with the Divine as an unlimited creation of God. Thus, they saw themselves as the image and likeness of God and not just a body, a persona, or an ego.

The key to remember as you read this book is that women who reported being *more spiritual* reported *less stress* and felt they had *more control* and were better equipped to transcend the work environment's negativity. They reported having a different understanding of the source of stress (ex: vibration) and a different way to respond—be still and know you are divine.

Women reported engaging in cleansing rituals, energy cleaning/clearing, or *cubicle conjuring* on the job. At home, they engage in burning rituals, chanting, mantras, ancestors and deity worship, divination, spiritual self-care, and daily spiritual practices.

This book reveals some, not all, of the spiritual resources, practices, and implements used for spiritual coping with work-related stress. I am sure this book will not scratch the surface of this topic, and some things mentioned may challenge or expand your understanding of spirituality or spiritual practices. Be open, and do not judge. Let's learn from these women. I assure you, there is more to know.

Black women in the United States have always worked and have always coped with work-related stress. From the plantation experience to the modern-day boardroom, PBW have always had to protect themselves from the vicissitude of work. There truly is nothing new under the sun. You may wonder how a co-worker is getting by in a hostile environment while you are floundering, and she is maintaining her center of calm. When you want to pull your hair out, maybe there is a resource she is tapping into that you are not. Perhaps she understands her life and her life's purpose a little differently than you. Maybe you should read on.

One of the symptoms of an approaching nervous breakdown is the belief that one's work is terribly important.
Bertrand Russell

3 CHAPTER 3

THE SOURCE

You and you alone are the source of your stress. Who else or what else could be? According to Lazarus and Folkman's (1982) theory, stress is external or existing outside of the individual. It is ubiquitous and is inescapable. Everyone is potentially vulnerable to stress. Stress is viewed as a negative punisher for those who succumb to it. There is nothing positive to gain from experiencing a stressor appraised as negative other than the decision to cope (see Figure 2). Coping in this model suggests you have accepted the stressor as a threat. You have to adjust yourself psychologically to manage the upset resulting from being exposed to the stressor. You may not be able to control negative stressors at work; however, coping means you have an appropriate response to the stressor given your resources for coping.

Spiritual Framework

From a spiritual perspective, the origin of stress is *internal*. Stress is attracted or magnetized to you by vibration. Furthermore, the experience of stress denotes misalignment with the "*God plan*" for your life. Stress is a positive teacher of what not to do. In this context, stress is not negative; rather, it is a messenger. It is a mirror reflection of old programs operating within your subconscious mind that are no longer serving you. Your job is to become aware.

Figure 2: The Spiritual Source of Stress: Mirror Reflection

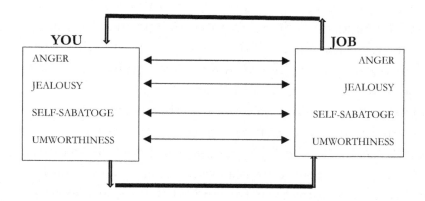

The Mirror

Can you argue with a mirror? If you were to look in the mirror right now and notice you had spinach in your teeth, what would you do? Would you argue with the mirror because it showed you an image of yourself with spinach in your teeth? Or would you use the mirror as a guide to remove the spinach and go on with your life? I am pretty sure you would do the latter. Jobs and the stress accompanying it acts as a mirror into the world of your subconscious mind. Your chosen profession is a mirror showing you precisely what is important to your ego. Is it judgment? Is it crime and punishment? Is it the intervention you never had as a child?

The second set of mirrors you encounter are the people on your job. They are great mirrors showing you exactly how you replicate your 0-7 "*what had happened story*" in your adult situations. Whether you believe it or not, there is no way a person would be in your orbit acting crazy if there was not a part of your mind that was equally crazy.

The What Had Happened Story

As a college professor, I trained many social work students to understand the client from a person-in-environment perspective (Dorfman, 2015). Understanding the client within his or her ecological system (ex. the family system) reduces shaming and victim-blaming because there is an understanding of the origins of the client's behavior. Similarly, your family dynamic is your first mirror or your "*what had happened story*." Your family and their drama show you exactly what your core issues are, what you are afraid of, what you are holding guilt for, and what to do if you desire to escape the vicious cycle of suffering. But what do you do? You probably decided to run as far away from your family as possible. You wonder how you could even be related to these people.

You convinced yourself that *they* are the ones with the problem, not you. If this was your situation, you probably left your family as soon as you could. You decided to put enough distance between you and them, believing this would solve all your problems. Not so.

If you left your family of origin to attend college, join the military, or enter the workforce, invariably you encountered, by attraction, individuals who match the exact vibration of your family. Why? Because this is YOUR vibration too.
The universe will provide you with ample opportunities to see yourself in the relationships you form with others outside

of your family. Most likely, they also share characteristics of your family. Every fault you find with these people is the fault you have to address within yourself. Your job is to acknowledge what you see in these human mirrors. It is information for correction. Next, your challenge is to do the spiritual work necessary to raise your consciousness to a higher level to escape this vicious cycle.

Without awareness or acceptance of the information from your mirrors, you will continue to externalize your experiences, point fingers, and accept no responsibility for your behavior. Even under high penalty, your ego will allow you to believe it is *them*, not you. <u>Workplace Voodoo</u> lets you know it is always you, and it can only be you. You are the one who is seeing and perceiving what is in the mirror, no one else. You can argue with the mirror or decide to clean it up. One choice leads to heaven, and the other choice keeps you trapped in a hell of your design.

The Development of the Ego

The experience of stress is an *effect* that has a *cause* and can only be experienced by the *egoic* mind. A healed mind cannot experience stress. The big question is, how did the egoic mind come about?

Psychologist Erik Erikson describes the ego's development in terms of crisis or challenges every soul coming to Earth must overcome to feel safe (Widick, Parker, and Knefelkamp, 1978). Life in the third dimension is about contrast. The birthing process is the first contrast the soul encounters upon arrival. When the *soul* left God/Source or the Divine expression of abundance and all-sufficiency, it had to quickly develop "*trust*" that this new world would love and support it as it was loved and supported by Source. Erikson's first developmental stage is called *trust vs. mistrust*. He posits to the extent the primary caretakers CAN respond in a timely and appropriate manner to the baby, the baby will develop *trust*. If the child's primary caretakers fail to provide abundant love or address its basic needs, *"mistrust"* or fear develops. Because the newborn soul knows it did not create itself, it also knows it is not responsible for itself. Distrust for this new world is the initial introduction of fear and vulnerability into the baby's subconscious mind.

Energetic Vibration

The baby does not have the mental capacity to understand its birth circumstances or to whom it was born. What the baby does understand and record in his or her subconscious mind is the energetic vibrations of these early childhood experiences. The ego is an aspect of your being created by the subconscious mind to store thoughts of fear, harm, or attack. Because fear is experienced energetically, the infant begins to attract situations reminiscent of the level of fear it perceived within its mind. For example, some babies are insatiable. They cry all the time regardless of whether they are well-fed, dry, and comfort, while other babies are quiet and easygoing. The more the baby mistrusts or believes it is separate from the everlasting Source that created it, the more vulnerable it will feel. When the environment does not respond to the newborn appropriately, it becomes increasingly terrified and accepts these thoughts of fear and terror as real.

Egoic Stress

The egoic mind is an illusion because God did not create it.

Your ego created it out of fear. God is love, and love does not know or understand fear. By now, your ego probably accumulated a Grand Canyon size repository for all of your fears (See Figure 3). It has complicated your soul's journey through life with this bag of fear and a belief in separation from God. This erroneous belief becomes the driving force for the ego to develop its survival plan.

Figure: 3

Fear/Love Continuum
Repository

FEAR---**LOVE**

-Need money	-Sharing
-Competition	-Cooperation
-Tradition	-Natural gifting
-Personal gain	-Greater good

Only this fearful part of your mind can show you a fearful, vengeful world—a world where threat and attack are possible. A world where revenge is expected, and protection are necessary. Listening to the ego and believing in its negative thoughts result in more fear. Fear is projected into your external world and presents as conflict and conflictual relationships. You think you must work for money. You hoard resources for yourself and your loved ones. You are less likely to share, especially the resources you determined are scarce. Sensing the lack and limitation of all resources, you become competitive as opposed to cooperative. You believe somewhere in your consciousness in a *"dog eat dog"* reality. You make sure you protect your interest and focus on your gain, not the good of all. You do not make life choices based on infinite possibilities. You make decisions based on tradition or family expectations, thus maintaining your version of the status quo.

Mind Projections

If you want to know what your ego is projecting, look carefully at your life. What do you see? What does your physical body look like? How is your health? What is the content of your personal and professional relationships? What does your bank account look like? Are you happy? Are you experiencing love in your life? When you are unaware of the truth of who you are, all areas of your life will be governed by your fearful egoic mind. When you come into the knowledge of who you are—an infinite and unlimited being, you see the virtue of sharing precious resources like time and attention, you cooperate with Spirit in co-creation. You focus and use your natural gifting to support you and not what schools have trained you to do. Love allows you to see yourself as part of humanity's greater good, not just a linear life beginning with birth and ending in death. Love is eternal, and so is every soul appearing temporarily on this Earth plane.

Mirror Reflections

Everything you attract on the job is a mirror reflection of what is stored in your egoic mind. Because the ego needs your corporation to survive, it must convince you that God called you to this profession. Since God did not create any profession, God cannot call you something He did not create. Your occupation became the justification for continuing down a path of pain and suffering mostly because you need the money. Your ego is so vested in dragging you everywhere, but the way you are supposed to go. The experience of pain is proof your ego has chosen external validations over the internal knowing you are the image and likeness of God. Because the ego operates entirely on its own, it can never know anything. It can only perceive based on erroneous data from the subconscious mind and the collective mass consciousness. Perception is not knowledge. All knowledge comes from God and is available to you at all times. You simply have to become aware of the truth of your divinity.

Detecting the Ego

The ego will make you exhausted. Employees are not exhausted from the work they perform. They are most likely exhausted from the barrage of negative, fearful, and attacking thoughts continually running through their mind all day long,

> *Did I email the report?*
> *Are they going to approve my vacation time?*
> *Do I have to go to this meeting?*
> *I'm running late. I hope I don't get fired.*
> *Did I leave the stove on?*
> *Is the boss coming into work today?*
> *I need to get off early.*
> *Is it too late to ask for time off?*

In these modern times, no one is performing arduous 17th-century labor. Nowadays, there are machines, gizmos, gadgets or doohickeys to perform these tasks. For the most part, working PBW are either sitting at a desk or doing very little physical activity on the job. There is very little evidence to justify the experience of exhaustion at the level it is expressed. Given these are your thoughts, you are responsible for recognizing what you are thinking. So, if you have capacity for unlimited thought, why on Earth would you deliberately choose thoughts of attack, fear, hate, anger or any type of negativity?

The function of the ego is vested in tricking you into thinking these thoughts are yours and they are real. This is the only way it can survive. Ultimately, the goal of the ego is to destroy you because it thinks it is separate from you. The ego does not realize that in trying to destroy you, it will also destroy itself. You may have heard of the saying,

Whoever dies with the most toys, wins.

Clearly, this represents the mindset of the ego. The ego does not recognize your divine purpose is to self-actualize and not just to accumulate temporary things (McLeod, 2007). No matter how many material things you may acquire, you end up becoming very physically exhausted and mentally drained on this path. Whatever you have acquired, will never seem to be enough. The ego is about comparison—*she who has the most toys wins,* compared to whom? Can you understand how some people who seem very well to do are also very miserable? Do you ever say to yourself,

If I had half of what they have, I would be set for life?

Seeking But Never Finding

These miserable rich people spend their lives seeking but never finding the thing that would fill this void. Because the material items being pursued are never going to fulfill your true purpose—The God Life. Thus, over lifetimes you grew increasingly frustrated, filled with anger, rage, and hatred. This became the picture you project into the world. You blame your selfish spouse, your greedy family, your self-absorbed children, your narcissistic boss, and your mean coworkers for everything you are experiencing. You do not understand why you are being treated so badly even though you are sacrificing everything to make sure you are a team player and doing everything to ensure everyone is happy.

Take Responsibility

When you do not take 100% responsibility for what you are out-picturing in your life, you will blame all others. You will always experience stress. Okay, how can you say that? Yes, you might have moved your family out of poverty by raising your social and economic status. Yes, you might have been the first in your family to go to college. Yes, you might be doing great financially, and the entire squad is benefiting from your hard work. However, the ego does not understand eternity. It is trapped in the limitation of time and space. Unbeknownst to you, you have been repeating this pattern of behavior for many lifetimes. The only reason why you are struggling on earth now is because you did not fix these issues in your previous lifetimes.

Reading this book may be the signal that perhaps you are ready to allow the real you to emerge to do the work. What does the outward picture of this look like? It looks like Robin Sharma, a former attorney who sold his home and his Ferrari to follow his soul's urge to the Himalayas and became a monk. It looks like a little girl, born to a single mother in Kosciusko, Mississippi, raised in poverty wearing potato sack dresses to become the richest African American of this generation and the first Black billionaire in North America.

Yes, Oprah Winfrey did that. It could look like you if you are willing to shed your ego and begin your fantastic soul journey to find out who you really are. Beware! On your soul journey, you must be courageous and steadfast. You must be willing to be humiliated by people you love, disowned by your family, degraded and jeered by your colleagues and perhaps shunned by the world you knew. If these things lead you to freedom, then you will understand a powerful teaching of the Christ,

> *But seek ye first the kingdom of God, and*
> *his righteousness; and all these things shall*
> *be added unto you (Matthew 6:33).*

And what are these things that shall be added to you? These are the everlasting things of God. It is peace of mind. It is abundance. It is the blessed assurance that all your needs are supplied according to God's idea of rich, not the Forbes List. It is living heaven on Earth. Your life will be miraculous.

Your Name

FYI, the only thing you own in this lifetime is your name. Employees are retiring at the highest rate ever and all they have to show for it is the passage of time and perhaps a collection of those plastic plaques and certificates of appreciation. In one or two generations from now, very few people will remember your names. How will you be remembered and for what? The toys and plaques you accumulated or the content of your good name?

The Body

On the physical level, the ego colludes with the body as its outward *energetic expression*. The body is merely a prop for showing you exactly what your mind is thinking. The late Dr. Masaru Emoto spent a large portion of his life studying the impact of vibration on water by examining the formation of water crystals exposed to various frequencies. Dr. Emoto used sound as the independent variable to look at the effects of low and high vibrational tones on water. When the water vials were exposed to high vibrational tones (ex. beautiful musical), magnificent crystals were observed with a microscope. When the water vials were exposed to low vibrational tones (ex. cacophony), the forming crystals were ugly and drastically less appealing.

Dr. Emoto's work has been replicated in many settings and consistently his research findings clearly demonstrate *vibration* (positive or negative) affects the human body. All thoughts are vibrational—negative or positive. Given we are roughly 76% to 80% water Dr. Emoto's research shows how your thought vibrations are key to understanding how your bodies respond to positive or negative thoughts you hold. For example, if high blood pressure shows up in your body, it is the result of low or negative vibratory thoughts. The egoic mind thinks it can have high blood pressure, so it produces it in the body.

Stress by Attraction

Understanding or better yet "*overstanding*" everything in your life is there by attraction. The ego guarantees you will have a "*what had happened*" story. Your fearful ego created this story in childhood between the ages of 0-7 in response to its perception of fear or threat of not being cared for. Your adult life is a replica of this story. It became the reason why you chose to dedicate your life to a particular profession—

one based on judgment, punishment, competition, evaluation, critique, comparison, or disbelief. Because this is your internal experience, you get to see it out-pictured or projected in the context of the workplace.

The Observer Self

Rap superstar and Bronx native, KRS-1, has an elegant method for demonstrating the difference between you and your egoic mind. In one of his lectures, he asked the audience to say the word "*rock star*" silently in their minds. Go ahead, you can try it. Say "*rock star*" in your mind. Did you say, "*rock star*"? Good! Let's play along. KRS-1 asked the audience to identify who said the word "*rock star*" in your mind? Who said it without using a mouth? Did you hear the word "*rock star*" in your head? Who heard it without using ears? He asked the audience to consider if they did not physically say "*rock star*" with their mouth, nor did they hear "*rock star*" with their ears, who was speaking and listening to the word "*rock star*"? It has to be some part of you. Obviously. From the spiritual perspective, this part of you is your soul or the "*observer*."

The "*observer-soul*" is the real you because it was created by God. This part of you exists in the backseat of your consciousness, watching everything you do. It is observing how the ego is controlling your life. Your soul should be in control. It should be leading you on a fantastic journey of adventure, one that tests the limits of your humanness, so you know without a shadow of a doubt you are more than a body—you are a divine being. The soul is incapable of experiencing fear, but the ego can. You have allowed the soul to sit in the backseat of your consciousness. The soul is waiting for you to wake up from the egoic nightmare and will allow it to sit in the driver's seat of your mind.

The Soul

The soul is the divine part of you. It is the eternal part of you that is actively trying to express itself. Your soul desires to lead you on a holy journey back to the only place it can go—back to God/Source/Divinity. Your soul wants to relieve you of accumulated guilt and remind you of your holiness—your pure and blameless God nature. It also desires to connect you with other high vibrational souls for spiritual growth and development. Your soul wants you to learn forgiveness, radical self-forgiveness. It wishes to release you from the suffering available in this world. Radical forgiveness is the realization that there is nothing to forgive. Everything happened to bring you to this point.

Your soul led you to this book. Somewhere in your mind, you desire to change. It is here right now. Workplace Voodoo shows you your insane egoic mind is the source of stress, nothing else. Once the ego is revealed, you have a choice. Keep doing what you are doing, and you will keep getting what you are getting. Or, you can choose to do something else—acknowledge your divinity and act accordingly.

Put the Ego to Work

The ego exists to show you what you are afraid of and what has been holding you back from rising to a higher spiritual level. Put your ego to work. Let it show you what you need to work on. Is it anger? Is it abandonment? Is it unworthiness? Reclaim the power you handed over to the ego. This is your real purpose on earth, not slaving at a job.

You have forgotten your way. The goal of <u>Workplace Voodoo</u> is to shine a light on the path back to your right mind—a mind of peace, love, and oneness. You are more significant than a job. You are magickal. Until you understand and accept your divinity, you will seek out jobs to validate your ego's story, and you will definitely experience job stress.

In my case, I chose to become a research scientist because this profession requires scrutiny, judgment, and critique. In actuality, I judged myself and opened myself up to external scrutiny, judgment, and critique. This was the takeaway from my *"what had happened" story* from my formative year. I could not perceive a world naturally loving me, honoring me, respecting me, and wanting me to do well. I could not imagine a world where my coworkers would cheer me on, were happy about my success, or where I was appreciated and treated fairly. This is what identification with the ego's *"what had happened story"* looks like.

The more I identified with the ego and not my divine identity, as God's creation, the more I was guaranteed to experience work-related stress. The mirror experience of stress was the evidence I believed what the ego was showing me was real. You can release yourself from this bondage by learning the lessons of the ego and evicting it from the driver's seat of your consciousness.

Everything is created twice, first in the mind and then in reality.
— Robin S. Sharma

4 CHAPTER 4

THE MIND

Professional Black women who reported being more spiritual than religious operate from a different mindset. Though they shared some core beliefs with religious women, the spiritual women understood themselves as an energetic being infinitely connected to everything in creation. Many have come into the understanding that they do not know the meaning of anything, especially the things they have given meaning to. They are open to redefining everything, to experience God's true intention for that thing. Look around you. Everything you see, you have given meaning to. Most likely, everything you see was already defined for you, and you go along with the program. Spiritual women create the mental space to entertain the possibility of a deeper meaning for everything they encounter.

Who Are You?

"Who are You?" An answer to this question is fundamental to the human experience, yet some never ask the question. Many more never seek the answer. Spiritual PBW repeatedly revisit the question of identity and are continually seeking the solution.

"Who do I have to become to effortlessly experience the delightful things in life?"

Spiritual women often revisit this question. They know they are ever-evolving, unlimited, and eternal. They are open to the process of transformation and expansion. Spiritual PBW know God's Spirit lives within them, and this part of their identity is eternal. It is impervious to and untouched by sin, judgment, pain, suffering, or death. As energetic beings, they believe in the transformation and transmutation of energy. There is no death, just transition. Thus, they believe in life after life, not life after death. Though initially, it may take her years to realize it, she eventually comes into this awareness and remembers she is not a body, she is not a name or label. She has awakened to the knowledge she is a divine creation of God powered by this same Spirit. It is the same for you. You are more significant than you allow yourself to be. You can do all things because your body is a temple. The Kingdom of God lives within you. This is proof of your holiness.

> *Don't you know that you yourselves are God's?*
> *temple and that God's Spirit dwells in your midst?*
> *(1 Corinthians 3:16)*

My Vegas experience (which you will read about in Chapter 11) pointed me toward exploring my spiritual identity. As smart as I believed myself to be, I could not answer a simple question like, *"Who are you?"* You may be fortunate to know who you are. However, this was not my experience. At the time, I did not know. I was caught up in my identification with a job title, degrees, status in someone's life, labels, and outside validation. I know now that I am a divine creation of God, made in His image and likeness. I am an ever-expanding and ever expressing God on Earth. Even now, in writing this book, I am evolving and transforming.

Since Vegas, I have traveled to highly spiritual places having spiritual experiences all over the world. My experience in the water temple in Bali washed me of religious ambiguity. I released myself from religious bondage and experience myself as the very essence of God. I am not afraid of death or the threat of hell used by the church to scare me into a religious box.

My Ayahuasca experience in the mountains of Peru showed me I could leave my body in this third dimension and travel to unlimited dimensions to connect with other spirit beings. I can meditate and take my soul anywhere in this vast universe outside of time or space. After five Ayahuasca rituals, I do not believe I can fly. I *know* I can fly.

I am embracing the spiritual identity of my Galactic Signature, *White (Electric) Mirror*. I wrote a poem based on the qualities and characteristics of White *Electric* Mirror and placed it in the front of this book. Stop. Go to the front of the book and read it. Reread it if you read it once already. You have a galactic signature too. I can help you find yours.

It took me almost three full years before the identity of *White Mirror* resonated with me. I had to raise the level of my consciousness to connect with that aspect of myself. After three years, I realized I am *White Mirror*. This spiritual identity captures my essence and life's path so precisely. You may have a similar experience when you learn to decode yourself. Spend some time with yourself and ask this simple question, *"Who am I?"*

Why Are You Here?

Spiritual Black women know they are here for a divine purpose. *"Thy will, not my will be done"* is accepted and understood. They understand God's plan has nothing to do with religion. God's plan is revealed step-by-step. You are here to execute the Divine plan for your life by having faith that the Creator who created you will never leave you nor forsake you. You are always connected to this Divine Source. Your job is to say *"yes"* only to the things God wants you to do. If God speaks to you and asks you to do something, do it. Do not ask too many questions. Asking questions is a function of the ego. It means you do not trust God or yourself. When you question what you hear from Spirit, you naturally delay execution. Time means nothing to God. It is always your choice how long it takes before you align with the God Plan for your life.

Co-Creating with God

Hopefully, you will get to the point where there is a more profound longing for the Divine things on Earth. Seek after it. Live for it. Know in your core there is something special God wants you to do in this lifetime. Commit to doing it. Spiritual PBW actively prepare themselves to be transparent vessels for co-creating with God. Most have realized the purpose they created for themselves in the work world is a sham and has led to pain and suffering. Many realized having great success, and material abundance left them with an empty feeling inside. In this unaware stage, you will continuously set out to satisfy some real or imagined need, typically outside of yourself.

You will continue to seek fulfillment, but probably never find it. This is the number one ego trick. The ego keeps you busy seeking happiness where it can never be found. You join so many clubs and organizations. You stay busy. So many people rely on you for everything, and you deliver each time no matter what. Ask yourself, is your plan working? Are you ignoring yourself? Spiritual Black women know to look within themselves for the answers. How? By spending time with themselves. Spiritual PBW know how to deeply appreciate themselves. They celebrate their uniqueness. They know God establishes their worth, not an award or prize for doing something. God is always inviting you to co-create. Create the works of art that are within you. Write your books. Sing your songs. Do those things that are inspired by God. The world is waiting for you to say "yes" to your co-creations.

Who is God?

As a little girl, I believed that God was an old grey hair, grey beard man who lived in the clouds like most around me. He was up there judging, punishing, and supposedly loving us all at the same time. I learned about God from a Judo-Christian perspective, as did most women in this study. I learned God was a male. He is *omnipresent*-He is everywhere. God is *omniscient*-He has ALL the knowledge. God is *omnipotent*-He has ALL the power.

So, who is God?

Spiritual women know God is the ALL. God is both male and female. God is everything you perceive. God is in everyone. Every time you encounter another soul, be careful how you treat them. You are having a godly experience.

For where two or three gathers in my name,
there am I with them (Matthew 18:20).

God and the Devil

Most spiritual PBW do not believe in a devil. They believe in God/Source/Higher Power/Universe. They believe in the polarity of light and dark energy. For example, angles have light energy, and demons, also angels, have dark energy. They understand the devil as a metaphor for the dark part of the mind-controlled by the ego. It is the place in your consciousness where you hide your shame, guilt... and any aspect of yourself you do not want to reveal to the world. This information is stored in the dark. Things that grow in the dark are mold, mildew, mushrooms, and your negative shadow self. There is no devil. There is only the part of your consciousness that requires light. Your spiritual journey prompts you to shed light on the mold and mildew of your awareness so you can clean it up and be restored to your right mind.

Religious Duality

The egoic mind believes in religious duality-good and evil, God vs. devil. If we observe this concept from a scientific perspective, God and the devil are clearly mutually exclusive variables. So, if God is omnipresent, where can a devil exist? If the devil cannot be anywhere God is, where does this devil live? If God is *omniscient*-knows EVERYTHING, what can the devil know? What can you really know outside of God's wisdom? If God has ALL the power, what power can a devil have? What ability do you have outside of God? Spiritual people take issue believing in the concept of a devil or nemesis of God. What kind of God has an arch-enemy or a birthday? Think about it. What kind of all-powerful God has time to fight with a devil? Can God even know evil? We can spend a lifetime on this topic. I suggest you decide who you want to give your attention to, an omnipotent God that is real or a story of a devil passed down to us by religion.

Relationship to Others

From a spiritual God-centered perspective, spiritual PBW believe they are the consciousness of God. They originate from the same stream of consciousness that created everything—God. Since God created everything, everything is an extension and expression of God. How can a created thing be anything else? Everyone and everything you encounter is God. This understanding of relationships is key to loving your neighbor as you love yourself.

Traditional indigenous spiritual beliefs incorporate the notion of God as the All—a Great Spirit permeating everything. They revere everything in the heavens and earth like the wind, water, fire, trees, rocks, plants, and animals because God created them. Spiritual PBW understand God as the All and understand everything they experience is an aspect of God. You are here to have as many God-like experiences as possible. Each experience expands your God-like consciousness and your God-like nature is that as an abundant creator.

Relationship to Environment

God is love. Your relationship with each other, your physical world, and yourself ideally should be one of love. Despite God giving you this beautiful planet as your home, human beings are continuously and constantly destroying it. We live in an era where humankind has created so many deadly toxic substances, and we expose ourselves and our tiny babies and pets to them every day.

Plastic is one of the deadliest substances on earth. It is almost unconscionable to know every single piece of plastic ever manufactured on earth still exists and is wandering around somewhere on the planet. Approximately 185 million pounds of plastic waste is discarded like trash in the United States each year. That accounts for a lot of water bottles! Can you imagine your life without plastic? Can you give up your dependence on plastic for a cleaner, better world? For many, the answer to this question is "Yes/No." Yes, we want a cleaner, better world, and, no, we are not willing to part with the modern conveniences of plastic.

Spiritual Responsibility

Many spiritual-minded individuals understand their responsibility to the planet. They are willing to reduce their carbon footprint by doing something as simple as using reusable water bottles and refusing single-use plastic containers. You can live in a cleaner, healthier world by taking personal responsibility for your spiritual relationship to the earth. Do your part and be an example for others to follow. Begin by cleaning up your immediate environment. Rid your home of toxic chemicals and products. Throw them out today and convert your home to a clean, non-toxic environment. Use the money you are currently spending on poisonous cleaning products and switch to natural botanicals. I made the switch and can attest it has made a difference in my body and my home.

Using biodegradable plant botanical and plant medicine is part of my spiritual gifting and practice. I can help you with this too.

Daily Spiritual Practice

Most spiritual Black women engage in consistent daily spiritual practice. A spiritual practice is anything you do that is enjoyable and brings you in closer communion with God. It can be early morning prayer, mediation, chanting, reciting Psalms, singing, dancing, yoga, a hot cup of herbal tea, or whatever gets your spiritual energy turned all the way up.

Spiritual practice can be as straightforward or as elaborate as you like. When I started my spiritual practice, I made a big deal about it. I wanted to impress myself. I would set my intention to rise early to pray and meditate. Yes, I would rise early...to turn the alarm off and go back to bed! I learned training my mind and body to engage in a daily spiritual practice was hard! It takes discipline and consistency to build up a daily spiritual practice.

Discipline comes when you DECIDE your body is not the boss of you. You can reclaim control over your mind that controls your body. All spiritual masters develop a daily spiritual practice that takes dominion over the stronghold the egoic mind has over the body. Getting up early or staying up late in daily spiritual practice has become natural as breathing to me. If I fall short of my goal, I simply pour love on myself and start the next day again. It will not benefit you or your spiritual journey if you are hard on yourself or if you constantly criticize yourself for not achieving your daily goals the first time. Be gentle to yourself and try again. Begin your spiritual practice today. Document it, so you will see how it is working out for you.

Above all else, guard your heart, for everything you do flows from it.
Psalms 4:23

5 CHAPTER 5

THE HEART

U nderstanding the purpose and function of the heart are essential to your spiritual growth and development. The heart is not just a physical organ in the body. It is also part of your spiritual composition. It is the connector between your physical self and God. Let's examine the physical side first. According to the Black Women's Health Imperative, Inc., an organization dedicated to educating the public about trends in Black women's health, among Black women 20 years and older, 49% have some type of heart disease or disorder! This means almost half the Black women in the United States are operating with a broken heart.

Causal Factors

How did this statistic come about? The research I conducted for my dissertation pointed to several causal factors like genetics, diet, socioeconomic status, educational level, historical, environmental, and on, and on, and on. I focused on the Black woman's identity as a "*worker*." I discussed how the context of slavery defined her role first as chattel property and compulsory laborer and during post-emancipation as identification with one of four distinct archetypes: The Mammy, The Jezebel, The Sapphire, and The Tragic Mulatta. The Civil Rights Movement of 1965 generated a fifth archetype, The Superwoman (Thomas, Witherspoon, and Speight, 2004).

The Mammy

The Mammy was an older, dark-skinned, obese, docile slave/employee whose role was put the needs of her White owner/employer before her needs and the needs of her family. This archetype is portrayed as loyal, obedient, and submissive to her owner/employer. The Mammy was a fixer. She knew how to fix any and every problem or situation that came up for her White family. She nursed their children and starved her own infant children. She was prized because of her loyalty and devotion to everyone but herself.

Modern day *Mammies* exist. They bring work home. They work over dinner, through birthday celebrations. They grade papers while they are supposed to be spending time with loved ones. They are absent from important family events due to work obligations. They are tired, overweight, and they feel obligated to keep going.

The Sapphire

The Sapphire is the post-emancipation archetype of the dominant, castrating Black woman wearing the pants in the family. She was an aggressive workhorse whose dominating characteristics were a turn off to Black men and her behaviors that usurped their role as protector and provider for the family. Unlike the Mammy, this archetype lacks maternal instincts and compassion for her family. She was a workhorse who competed on the same level as Black males.

Some social scientists believed modern-day Sapphire behavior produced the increasing number of Black female-headed households. Without the balance of a man or father in the home, Sapphire's children are allegedly less academically capable and have a higher risk of criminality (Sampson and Wilson, 1995).

The Jezebel

Primarily culturally incompetent, culturally imperialistic White Christian missionaries who first encountered continental African women created this archetype. Unaccustomed to African women's culture, White Christian men and women perceived the African women they encountered as uncivilized, with an insatiable animalistic sexual desire. African women were viewed as promiscuous and sexually immoral beings who needed to be saved by Christianity. This belief was carried over to the plantations and projected onto Black women.

The Jezebel and The Mammy are polar opposites. On the one hand, White society viewed the Black female worker as simple-minded and loyal, and at the other extreme, they were cunning and conniving. They were willing to sleep her way to the top.

The modern Jezebel archetype is portrayed as harsh and impervious to pain. She is incapable of compassion towards others, especially the Black man. She is slick and not to be trusted, especially on the job.

The Tragic Mulatta

In addition to being subjected to the Southern plantation's

atrocities, Black women produced children through rape by their slave masters. Sexual exploitation and abuse were the most profound expressions of Black women's complete subjugation during this era (Bacchus, 2002). The offspring of the slave master and the Black woman was proof of their sexual activity.

The Tragic Mulatta challenged any claim of endogamy or racial purity among Whites. As such, these women are called tragic. These women presented phenotypically as White and capable of passing for White in the work world. However, the *"one-drop rule"* of African blood made it impossible for her to fully enjoy a White woman's freedom because she was still categorized as Black. Yet her physical features helped *The Tragic Mulatta* get ahead in the work world faster than her darker skinned sisters.

Advancement in *The Tragic Mulatta* career depended upon her employers and/or co-workers never finding out her secret. She shuns her Black roots and looks down upon her darker-skinned sisters. They see her as unsympathetic and deceptive. If her true racial identity was revealed, both the White and Black communities would shun her as well. She would have nowhere to turn for support. Hence, the tragedy.

The Superwoman

The most recent archetype germane to working Black women are the archetype of the Superwoman or the Strong Black Woman. The Superwoman woman is a composite of various aspects of each stereotypical model described above. The Mammy is similar to the Martyr archetype; however, regarding Black women, the modern-day Mammy takes care of everyone on the job. She works late and takes on extra assignments to the detriment of her health and well-being. She is neglectful of her own husband and children to take care of things at the office. She brings her work home.

The Sapphires are the problem Black women, also known as the "*Bitch*." They are the kick-ass, no-nonsense Black women who are quite scary. No one likes this lady. Her co-workers defer to her out of fear. Allegedly, like The Jezebel, she slept her way to the top. She made power moves using sex and sexuality, not her education or intelligence, to advance her career. If she happens to be light enough in completion, she, like the Tragic Mulatta, could pass and become part of the inner circle, yet she must endure the jeers of race abandonment from her peers.

The Superwoman puts up a front of strength, but it is a fragile veil. Because of her top-ranking position in the company, she is expected to be grateful. She is to do all and be all to everyone all the time. This facade prevents her from ever fully expressing her true creative desires. She is often in psychological distress yet unwilling to address these needs for fear of appearing weak. Unfortunately, most Black women in the workplace are still judged by these stereotyped identities, which were created for them based on the history of White oppression of Black women.

Moving Over Mobility

Regardless of educational attainment, talent, or skill, Black women's mobility up the economic ladder traditionally occurred only after White women moved out of a lower rank and on to more prestigious positions (Bacchus, 2002). An example of this *"moving over"* phenomenon is the economic structural pattern established during the industrial revolution and beyond when women began entering the paid workforce (Pollard, 1963). This pattern remained even after the Civil Rights Movement of 1965. Job opportunities for all minorities improved, yet professional Black women remained in lower status white-collar jobs. In comparison, the higher status white-collar jobs continue to be available to only White males and Whites women (Bacchus, 2002).

The Identification

In my initial review of the literature, I discussed coping with work-related stress as the ability to manage stressors linked to complex cognitive and behavioral processes associated with coping outcomes—problem-focused or emotion-focused (Bacchus, 2002). However, upon learning about the spiritual source of stress, I am willing to abandon the numerous causal factors I studied voraciously and meticulously outlined for my research study. I am ready to accept one causal factor—identification.

How and what you have chosen to identify with is at the heart of the matter. Who are you? What have you chosen to identify with?

Have you chosen to identify with a degrading stereotype or the image and likeness of God?

Who do you believe yourself to be in your heart of hearts?

Are you a castrating bitch or a creation of the Divine?

The more you deny your divinity, the more prone you will be to fall into the identification trap. This trap was set for you hundreds of years ago on a distant plantation. Ask yourself:

How do I show up to work?
As a child of God or as a stereotyped archetype?

The Heartbroken

On a metaphysical level, if the mind is in cahoots with the body, then the heart is the master of the mind (Lea, 2018). The heart, which is an electromagnetic phenomenon, regulates your emotions. Your emotional status is communicated to the brain, and the brain then displays it energetically on the body. Why are half the Black women in the United States suffering from heart disease? Because metaphysically, they are heartbroken. They think they are one of these degrading archetypes when they are genuinely a Divine spark of God. The moment you begin to dissolve the painful identity inherited from the plantation and identify with your divinity, you create a path to healing first for yourself and then for your sisters. I intend to heal my broken heart by meditating on Psalms 34:18:

The Lord is close to the brokenhearted and
saves those who are crushed in spirit.

I *heart* you!

To help people you must first start with yourself.
—Shanna Star

6 CHAPTER 6

THE LEVELS

Central to the concept of spirituality is the idea of consciousness. Your consciousness or awareness of an aspect of yourself that is the soul is another means to answer the question,

Who am I?

Exploring your consciousness allows you to know which part of your mind you identify with most, the ego or the divine. As a human being, your humanness represents your fleshly nature, ruled by the five senses, and controlled by your fearful, destructive ego. Your beingness is represented by Christ consciousness or the God-like nature of your soul. In this context, Christ is not a persona, but a title of distinction is given to denote an enlightened being.

God Consciousness

Christ or God-consciousness is not a religious principle. It is a spiritual principle. It is the process of diminishing your ego so your soul may awaken to the knowledge you are God's genetic offspring. By divine design, the only thing you can ever be is the image and likeness of God. Every soul comes to earth with this jewel buried deep within its *being* consciousness. Christ consciousness is the inner awareness you are more than your physicality, and you have an undeniable yearning to seek your true god-like nature. The process of doing so means you must learn how to shift your mind from your current consciousness level to a higher level of consciousness.

The Ego's Function

The primary function of the ego is to keep you stuck in your humanness. Your human consciousness keeps you on a mental hamster wheel of endless repetition. It does so by controlling your thoughts. The ego has manufactured all the ideas it wants you to have. It regurgitates the same 80,000 thoughts each day such that your today tends to look exactly like the day you had yesterday. Your thoughts create the world you see. If you do not change your thoughts or replace old thoughts with new ones, your life will look exactly the same day in and day out.

If you observe this in your life, it is because the ego is running your life, and one day you will look up and realize 20 years have passed you by. Until you challenge or replace these thoughts and set out on a self-remembrance journey, you will go nowhere. You will never find your way back to your original identity-God consciousness.

Self-Determination

As a human, you have the right to self-determination. Nonetheless, your mind, governed by the ego, invariably will

50

lead you on a path far from the way back to God. It will make choices for you and convince you they are your choices. Most of these choices are contrary to the God-like nature of your soul. You are responsible for making *all* the conscious decisions for your life and no one else.

The Prodigal Son

The Bible provides a perfect case study of this phenomenon. The Prodigal Son in Luke 15:11-24 describes the stages of your soul's journey. First, as divine beings of love and light, The Prodigal Son was one with its Source-God. Then, through the entrance into the third dimension-Earth and identification with the ego, The Prodigal Son made numerous choices resulting in the accumulation of negativity and karma in his consciousness. As anger, shame, guilt, unforgiveness, and hatred accumulated, The Prodigal Son began observing his fallen position. He began to experience a deep sense of unworthiness. Life became so painful for him that he was willing to eat slop with swine.

One day, during his most profound dismay, his soul awakes to remind him of his divine identity. He realizes he is the son of a King. He DECIDES to make his journey back to his Father, despite the ego's admonitions and jeers. When he approaches his Father's kingdom, The Prodigal Son finds his Father, the King, rushing out to meet him. The king orders a big celebration. The King did not care what The Prodigal Son did. The King was too busy being happy his son had returned. The King orders a grand celebration. He dressed his son in the most beautiful raiment and forgave him completely. Finally, the Prodigal Son is back in his rightful place in the kingdom—at the right side of his Father.

This is the process all souls undertake to be restored to its rightful place in the Kingdom of God. The life of Jesus, the Christ provides another archetype of the soul's journey back to God. Jesus said,

> *I am the way and the truth and the life.*
> *No one comes to the Father except through me.*
> *(John 14:6)*

Jesus came to the third dimension to teach and explain Universal Law to the religious-minded. He became an example to show you how you can be healed of your destructive mind. He came to inform you about your manifesting power. He revealed that through a relationship with God, the ALL you have a path to self-forgiveness.

> *Very truly I tell you, whoever believes in me will do the works I have been doing, and they will do even greater things than these, because I am going to the Father.*
>
> *And I will do whatever you ask in my name, so that the Father may be glorified in the Son.*
>
> *You may ask me for anything in my name, and I will do it (John 14:12-14)*

The archetype of Jesus shows you how to give up the old destructive thought patterns of your ego to find your way back to God/Source/Heaven—life and life more abundantly.

> *The thief (the ego) cometh not but to steal and to kill and to destroy. I am come that they might have life, and that they might have it more abundantly (John 10:10).*

To the extent you are willing to relinquish identification with your ego and identify with your soul's light, you create a path to a higher level of consciousness. The journey to raise your level of consciousness begins with a decision to change your mind. You and only you can change your mind from egocentric to God-centered. You have to let go of the ego's destructive negative thoughts and replace them with the knowledge that the God who created you is not the author of fear.

Self-Worth

God established your self-worth according to His unlimited abundance and not by the narrow categories created by society (e.g., college professor, lawyer, doctor, governor, president, lieutenant, etc.). The ego uses its many tactics to trick you into believing you are limited and not worthy of an expansive life. It convinces you that identifying as a job title is exactly who you are. If you cannot accept your beauty and intrinsic self-worth, you are guaranteed to experience stress. Stress rises because your ego places your self-worth in everything outside of yourself (e.g., jobs, relationships, titles, money, and material possessions, etc.) and not where it belongs—CONNECTION to Source.

Spiritual Development

I am so grateful for the work of Dr. Michael Bernard Beckwith for providing a model for understanding stages of spiritual development. His four levels of consciousness will help you to explore and answer the big question,

Who am I?

A Stage Approach

Dr. Michael Bernard Beckwith's Levels of Consciousness uses a staged approach to spiritual development and unfolding (Minevalley, 2018). In this regard, spiritual development occurs in the orderly movement from one distinct level of consciousness to another. Observation of spiritual developmental change is characterized by observed qualitative differences in behavior. Dr. Beckwith describes *four* levels of consciousness or stages of spiritual development:

1. *To me*;
2. *By me*;
3. *Through me*;
4. *As me*.

Progression through each level may take years or many lifetimes. These stages are nonlinear, meaning you may experience numerous turns and twists on this path, or you may not always understand why you had a particular experience. However, Dr. Beckwith's framework is a great tool to gauge progress on your journey to spiritual enlightenment by observing your experiences—pain and suffering or joy, peace, and abundance.

Table 1. provides details on Dr. Beckwith's Levels of Consciousness. I included my study variables (locus of control and spiritual opportunity) by adding a column to the table's left. This table allows you to assess yourself in terms of

(a) *orientation to self*-who you believe yourself to be;

(b) *locus of control*—how much power you think you have over your life;

(c) *the prevailing spiritual* question at that level: *"Why are things always happening to me?"* and

(d) *spiritual opportunity*-from pain to bliss.

This framework will help you to understand where your consciousness is now as you awaken more and more to your "Soul's journey."

Table 1: Levels of Consciousness

	Stage 1 To Me	Stage 2 By Me	Stage 3 Through ME	Stage 4 As Me
Orientation to Self	Victim	Ego	Channel	One
Locus of Control	External	External	Internal	Oneness
Prevailing Question/ Challenge	Why are things always happening to me?	I am in control. I am the captain of my ship.	I am a clear vessel of God/Spirit / Source	I and the Father are One
Spiritual Opportunity	Pain Suffering	Exhaustion Enlightenment	Satisfaction Love	Bliss Love

Level 1 Victim Consciousness

Who am I?

If you believe you are a body with a name, personality, belief system inherited from your family, and the broader social environment, you should be terrified. In fact, on a subconscious level, you are. At Level 1 Victim Consciousness, your orientation to self is that of a victim. You believe things are happening to you and you have no control to stop it. You are not ready or willing to take full responsibility for your life. You may find yourself being attacked or defending yourself against attack. You are always in combat readiness mode. You are still putting out fires on the job and at home. You live a painful life, and it shows up as physical health problems (ex. disease and physical deterioration) or mental health problems (ex. stress, anxiety, despair). Despite all the signs, you willingly continue on this path, hoping and believing if you work harder, or do more, or try to control the outcome, you will be fine. You can handle it. Not so. The opportunity provided for spiritual growth at this level is pain. Pain is a great motivator to find solutions. At Level 1 Consciousness, you are destined to feel not only pain, which is endemic to the human experience, but intense, prolonged suffering. The Bible says,

> *Beloved, I wish above all things that thou mayest prosper and be in health, even as thy soul prospereth (3 John 2).*

God wants your soul to prosper and be in good health. If you are working or putting your energy into an activity that is killing you (slowly), this scripture lets you know clearly, this path is not God's plan for your life. *Level 1 Victim Consciousness* is rigged to kill you. The ego is entirely in charge and is making all the decisions, ultimately leading to more pain and more suffering.

Level 2 Manifestation Consciousness

If you want to live a happy, fulfilled life, it is impossible to remain at *Level 1 Victim Consciousness*. You must level up. As you grapple with the question,

Who am I?

At *Level 2 Manifestation Consciousness*, you decide you are no one's victim. You begin seeking solutions to the problems and the negative issues showing up in your life. At this level of consciousness, you believe things are happening not *"to me"* but *"by me."* You are the captain of your ship. You begin to use your mind and spiritual principles to tap into your creative reservoir for your manifestations. Suddenly, the dark clouds lift, and you feel an intense desire to go after the life you really want. Spiritual teachers show up in your life. Spiritual books, like this one, appear in your path. You voraciously read. You begin to make connections with other people already doing the things you desire. Things are looking much, much better. You feel a sense of hope.

A Change in Squad

One key indicator you are at *Level 2 Manifestation Consciousness* is all your unessential relationships begin to disappear. Yes, dear. That inconsiderate, troublesome, selfish boo will disappear into the ether. Disruptive family members will exit your life. Certain people will not want to be around you. They will say, *"You changed."*

Good! As innocuous as you think they are, relationships no longer serving you or bringing you joy will disappear. Your opportunity for spiritual growth on the high end of *manifestation consciousness* is enlightenment. This end brings the most joy and appreciation to your life. On the low end of *manifestation consciousness* is exhaustion.

The ego is still in control because it does not want to go away. The ego is right there, ready to level up with you. If you are not aware, your ego will have you running around joining women's empowerment groups; volunteering for everything, selecting a disease to run, walk, or bike for; climbing mountains, run marathons, writing books, etc.

On the positive end, you set loving boundaries and end hurtful relationships. You begin egalitarian relationships with like-minded peers. You begin to expand your consciousness by believing you can overcome the negativity in your life by manifesting whatever you want. And you do. Things are starting to look better. People are coming to you for advice. They admire your courage. You are still somewhat attached to your *"what had happened"* story. You are using it as an example of how you flipped its negativity into positivity to push ahead. You have transmuted the pain of your *"what had happened"* story into pearls of wisdom.

Level 3 Channel Consciousness

At *Level 3 Channel Consciousness*, all the productive work done on the high end of Stage 2 becomes the foundation of your real purpose. You recognize things are happening *through you.* Now, you have an inner subjective belief your life is *for you,* not *against* you. There is nothing out to get you. Increasingly, you are becoming a vibratory match to the things you want in your life, and this is why you are always being blessed. You are finding out the universe has wonderful treats for you. You are a manifesting vessel. Something unusual is always happening in your life, and you have learned to surrender to this energy. At this stage, your new normal is miracles. You are aware of the divine operating through you to manifest things you could not have conceived outside your present level of consciousness. This Bible verse says it precisely,

Eye has not seen, nor ear heard,
Nor have entered into the heart of man
the things which God has prepared for
those who love Him (1 Corinthians 2:9).

Who am I?

At *Level 3 Channel Consciousness,* you realize you have the power to still your mind long enough to hear from God/Source/Higher Power, and you are willing to take directions from this Source. You have moved away from the *muggles.* Your life is magickal. You found a more elegant way of producing the results you want in your life. Your connection with your spiritual core is stronger than ever. You can access and command the quantum—the invisible, intangible world where the formless begins to form. You develop your daily spiritual practice through prayer and meditation. You prepare your mind to be a clear channel for infinite possibilities. You realize as Jesus did,

It is no longer I who lives, but it is
Christ who lives in me. (Galatians 2:20)

You are becoming unfuckwithable!

Level 3 Channel Consciousness gives you your spiritual position for manifestation. It is found in Matthew 6:10:

***Thy** kingdom come, **Thy will** be done.*

Thy Will

When your will aligns with *Thy will,* you are surrendering to your divine purpose. Not your will, but God's will is what

59

you are doing on earth—or God's plan, not the plan you made up in *Level 1 Consciousness*. The issue here is having clear intentions.

People often pick up causes, issues, and problems, firmly believing that God created them as the intervention for these causes, concerns, and difficulties they experienced in childhood. For example, you may think you are the voice for the voiceless, the protector of the weak and defenseless. You believe your purpose on earth is to be a relief to those in pain, and into pleasure through your earthly good works.

I understand this mindset because this mindset led me to choose a career as a social work professor. I cannot remember what I wrote in my admission essay. I can only imagine it was a *"what had happened"* story about how I suffered as a child, rose above the pain to do well academically, and become a university professor who got fired and found her divine path. Now my life's goal is to help other people do the same, hopefully with less drama.

Ironically, my research interest at that time was *"intimate partner abuse among college-educated Black women."* My subconscious drive was to be the intervention for brilliant women who were kicking ass on the job and getting their asses kicked at home—like me, like my mother, and like so many other highly intelligent women I encountered. I wanted to unravel what I felt was the biggest question mark in my mind—

"Why did I, with all the sense the good Lord gave me, allow violence to continue to reside in my life?"

At this level of consciousness, I realized the best intervention for this situation is *self-forgiveness* and *mind healing*. Forgive yourself for believing an illusion about yourself. Forgive yourself for thinking something happened to you that never did. Forgive yourself for holding on to a story, an old program that is not serving you. When you dwell in self-forgiveness long enough, you will be able to heal your mind of destructive thoughts trapping you in destructive cycles. You will recognize your healing when the people, places, and things that used to trigger you are looked upon with love and compassion. At this level of consciousness, I was able to break the cycle of intimate partner violence in my life. My desire is for my daughter to never experience what my mother, grandmother, great-grandmother, and I had to endure.

Accept Your Divinity

The joy of *Level 3 Channel Consciousness* is you are indeed an inspiration to many. You are no longer tossed around by external events. You have accepted your divinity which opens you up to the spiritual opportunity of satisfaction and love. People adore and respect you for your beingness, your very essence. You are recognized for your benevolence and consistent body of work. Your reward is the experience of God's grace and favor in your life. You are sowing good seeds and reaping a harvest of satisfaction, bliss, and abundance. Life is like a dream. Your friends and family cannot understand what you are doing to experience so much wealth. They think you are crazy and call you names behind your back.

In my case, I was having the experience of being called a fake doctor by family members. I felt I was being ridiculed and put down by their judgment of my Soul's journey. At first, I wanted to *"snap back"* because the people were saying these things, I felt, were not qualified to judge me! However, in this new mind space, I can process all information coming before me as information *for me.*

Being called *fake* was the signal for me to examine what kind of doctor God really called me to be. It made me question whether I dare to answer this call. I trained as a university professor and that is just one part of me. Through my journey, God has shown me my real identity. I am a healer. I am a metaphysical doctor. I use plant medicine to heal and restore the body temple. I have spiritual gifts of palmistry *clairalience*, I can smell into the spirit world. I can detect disease on people even before they get a formal diagnosis. I do not know why I have this ability. I just know I do...for God's purpose, not mine.

My physiological response to events lets me know where my level of consciousness is located at all times. If my knees start shaking because of something God wants me to do or if I am so afraid of what "they" and "them" will say, I know I am on the right path. At Level 3, you won't give a damn what anyone thinks or feels about you and your life. You are a vessel and your higher Self is finally in the driver's seat of your life.

Level 4 Being Consciousness

At *Level 4, Being Consciousness,* you manifest everything *"as me."* The false line of separation between yourself (ego) and your divine self (God) is dissolved. You feel oneness with self and Source. There is no separation or feelings of disenfranchisement between you and the Creator as with *Level One: Victim Consciousness.* There is only integration. As a creative being, you have the power to create anything in your life, and you usually do. At *Level 4 Being Consciousness,* you are a conscious co-creator with God. You are what God is doing on earth. Your creative imagination is high, and you are a powerful vibrational match to that which you want to manifest using Universal Law.

Who are you?

At Level 4, your life circumstances have pushed you to dig deeper into yourself and who you really are. You find yourself expressing yourself as the real authentic you. You need not do anything to *be.* You are no longer striving. You know without a shadow of a doubt that you are God personified.

I am that I am.

This is your new identity. You are unapologetically you. You are no longer looking externally, you know the kingdom of God lives within you, and you have access to how to create heaven on earth. Again, Psalm 82:6 reminds you:

You are "gods"... you are all sons of the Most High.

Those of a lower level of consciousness cannot fathom being God's expression and expansion on earth. They can never call themselves God. Not you! Although the scripture is clear, you are all sons of the Most High; lower-level consciousness will have them reinterpret this scripture to mean everything other than what it says—you are God. Jesus tells you in John 14:12-14:

Very truly I tell you, whoever believes in me will do the works I have been doing, and they will do even greater things than these, because I am going to the Father.

And I will do whatever you ask in my name, so that the Father may be glorified in the Son.

You may ask me for anything in my name, and I will do it.

At Level 4, you know unequivocally you are a spiritual being having a human experience. Some examples are Mother Teresa, Maya Angelou, Oprah, Beyoncé, and Michelle Obama. None of these women have to do anything to be who they are. Generations of people will remember these *"beings"* because of their impact on the world. Getting to this level of consciousness may take a lifetime or many lifetimes. Keep going, and eventually, you will arrive at a place of knowing deep down inside that you are an eternal divine being having a temporary human experience. More importantly, you no longer punch a clock or are alarmed from your sleep to go to a job. God is ordering your footsteps, and you have submitted to His path.

It helps if you remember that everyone is doing their best from their level of consciousness. Deepak Chopra

7 CHAPTER 7

LEVEL UP

You may be wondering what levels of consciousness have to do with work-related stress or <u>Workplace Voodoo</u>? My short answer is EVERYTHING. At some point in your lifetime, either this one or the next, you might desire to experience unimaginable joy. You may want to connect with your higher self, the self, which is divine and magickal. Who is this self? This is the self that is always with you. The self that sees you without eyes hears you without ear- and touches you without hands. <u>Workplace Voodoo</u> operates in this realm—the unseen, the mystical, and the magickal. For highly spiritual women, this world is more real to them than the physical world they live in now. Dr. Bernard Beckwith defines magick as,

"...what you do to intentionally cause transformation in your life."

Workplace Voodoo is spiritual awareness. It is everything you do to cause your negative subconscious mind to step aside long enough to reprogram it to deliver to you your exact desired effect. Thus far, my spiritual journey required me to *"know my self."* Now, I am specifically being called to *"know my spiritual Self."* One way to remember my spiritual self is to discover my level of consciousness.

Who am I?
Who do I believe myself to be in relation to my outer
experience?
Can I be my authentic self, or do I have to "code switch"
to avoid critique?

You can ask yourself,

"What type of relational experiences am I currently
having on the job?"

Are these experiences harmonious or conflictual? Do you get along with co-workers, or are you the one always in conflict with others? As for me, I never set out to cause trouble or friction on the job. I always thought I was doing well, but somehow my name would be caught up in conflict and drama or *"conflama"* as my coach calls it. I would always be left wondering,

"How did I get here? How did this happen?"

I always did well in my duties. I was checking off all boxes-excellence in teaching, service, and research. *What was I doing wrong?* I was told success in academia required *"ass-kissing,"* and I was unwilling to do that. Who knows? Maybe that was it? Barring *"ass-kissing,"* I could not understand what was going on around me, and once again, I felt powerless. Years later, I was introduced to Dr. Beckwith's work on *levels of consciousness*, I understood everything I was experiencing originated in *my* consciousness. Yes, my mind, no one else's. If I was undergoing scrutiny or judgment, it was because I was scrutinizing and judging myself. I was simply replicating situations on the outside to match what I was experiencing on the inside. Lack of awareness is what characterizes *Level 1 Consciousness (Victim)*— *"things were happening to me."*

I experienced this on the job over and over again. I thought I just had to find a job that was a better fit for me. I still felt the problem was outside of me. Clearly, everything that was happening to me on the outside originated inside my consciousness. Therefore, this is where the changes needed to be made. The way my mind was set up in *Level 1,* everyone was out to get me on the job-everyone and everything. I believed there was something around every corner, ready to jump out and get me.

With this consciousness, I attracted more and more negativity playing the victim role in each scenario. *The Victim* was in all my intimate relationships too. At *The Victim* level of consciousness, suffering became a self-fulfilling prophecy. Also, *The Victim* made sure I chose men who were incapable of loving me. At one point in my life, I allowed a man to beat me, hurt me, not care for me on any level, disrespect me with side chicks, and not take care of our child. This person was capable of love and being responsible, but just not to our child or me. In addition to my *Inner Victim,* my *Wounded Child* popped up to remind me that I would never get what I truly wanted, and suffering *is* my normal.

During my academic tenure, my ego thought it was a good idea for me to *"fight for my rights."* I wrote letters, went to Affirmative Action, lodged complaints, used big words, quoted policies, and begged for fairness. I was appalled no one in the administration was interested in my issues. I engaged in numerous long, drawn-out back and forth email writing campaigns, I attended countless meetings that left me feeling physically exhausted with no resolution in sight. I felt mentally strained. All of these events took me further and further away from what I wanted to experience-bliss. I wanted to feel my work mattered to my students, the university, and myself. I believed I had to work hard using my creative energy to execute the university's vision and, in return, I would receive a salary and public recognition, the mark of success in academia. I was successful. However, when the day was over, I was emotionally depleted. I was resentful because all the good I was doing was not reducing the negativity or stress I was experiencing. So, at *Level 1 Victim Consciousness*, everyone and everything did get me. Most times this perception of constant attack fueled my exit from these professional appointments.

At Level 2, I felt I could make a difference in my life if I took control of my emotions and actions. I remember one point in my pre-conscious spiritual journey around 1992, I had the opportunity to briefly reconnect with someone I knew from my undergrad years. He was from Cornell University and was studying law at Howard University. I was going through a tough time in my life (as usual), and I began to tell him the gory details of my dreadful life. He looked up from his work and asked me to repeat these words:

> *"If it is to be, it is up to me."*
> *"If it is to be, it is up to me."*
> *"If it is to be, it is up to me."*

He told me I was responsible for my life and everything in it. This was the first time I realized I was the constant variable in all the drama found in my life. I was the *cause*, and the drama was the *effect*. I was reaping precisely what I was sowing.

From that point on, I began to redefine what I wanted in my life and its purpose. I began to seek after the things I felt would bring me joy. I made lists. I enrolled in graduate school. I got saved. I joined *Toastmasters*. I reactivated my gym membership. I volunteered. I became an Eastern Star. I sat on several Board of Directors. I was elected to an international committee serving women in West Africa. I went here. I went there. I did this and I did that. I was a great manifester. I received many intangible and tangible rewards--professional respect, validation, houses, new cars, money, travel, and fancy expensive things. I won awards and the recognition I desired, yet I still did not have the inner experience of bliss in my life.

On the lower end of *Level 2 Manifestation Consciousness,* I experienced exhaustion because I always believed I had to do all these things to manifest the life I desired. With all my *"do doing,"* I felt depleted and run down. I was doing way too much. Something had to give because I could not give anymore. I was always tired. I felt I was back at square one, but I had nicer stuff and fantastic opportunities. Eventually, I quit everything. I found out *"do doing"* was not the way for me. It was merely just another phase in my quest to move to a higher level of consciousness. Getting exhausted, feeling I was doing too much, and not being blissfully happy was the signal it was time to level up. Again.

As I move along my humble quest for spiritual enlightenment, peace, joy, love, happiness, and abundance, I have documented my leveling up process. I know where I have been, and I know I am not there anymore. I also know God divinely gave me the task of writing this book for you. Some parts of this book I clearly know did not come from my current level of consciousness. During my Bali retreat experience, my coach introduced me to channeling and showed me how to allow Spirit to write this book for you. I said a prayer and sat in meditation. I asked God,

"What would you have me write?"

I wrote exactly what came through me from God to these pages.

Ase!

Everything happens according to the law; chance is but a name for law not recognized, but nothing escapes the law." The Kybalion

8 CHAPTER 8

THE LAW

Professional Black Women who reported being more spiritual than religious venture beyond religious obligation and dogma to discover themselves within the larger cosmos. As such, they study Universal Law for its wisdom and practical application to their lives. Alignment with Universal Laws can help you understand and possibly transcend difficulties you are facing on the job. There are three immutable principles, meaning these laws are absolute and cannot change and four mutable laws, meaning they are transitory and are experienced by your understanding of the law and its application to your life. Mutable also means you can transcend the principles of these laws by choice to create your ideal reality. The goal is to master each of these seven Universal Laws for personal and spiritual growth and development. These laws help you understand how the universe or natural laws really work. It also provides you with a course of action for self-mastery.

The Law of Mentalism

The first immutable Universal Law is the Law of Mentalism. This law states the entire universe is mental. Everything in your entire Universe exist in your mind. All thoughts are created in with this mind, and all things manifest from this mind. Basically, all creation exists in your mind. Your physical reality is a manifestation of the inner thoughts of your mind. The Law of Mentalism reminds you that your divine power is to use this mind to create. It would behoove you to ONLY hold those thoughts in mind of the things you want to see actualized in your life.

Master teacher, Dr. Carolyne Isis Fuqua, says thoughts are like seeds. If you want sweet fruit, then you have to plant sweet seeds (thoughts). Do not be surprised when you end up with squash when you really wanted strawberries. And yes, if you are experiencing squash, but expecting strawberries, there must be an error in your mind. You were thinking squash when you really wanted strawberries.

If you are planting the wrong thought seeds, it is your responsibility to plant the right seeds. Your mind is always creating. Thus far, it has created everything in your life— right, wrong, and the unexpected. The great thing about the law of mentalism is if you do not like what you have created, you can use this same mind to create something else. Again, there is nothing that could happen outside of your mind. It is all you!

The Law of Correspondence

The Law of Correspondence is the second immutable Universal Laws. It states:

As above, So below; As below, So above;
As within, so without; As without so within.

Ok, so what does this mean? As above refers to the heavens, universe, or the macrocosm. The below refers to the Earth, your physical body down to the most minute cell or particle, or the microcosm. You, as your own microcosm or human souls is inextricably connected to the macrocosm-the universe or the Source of creation. The *"the within"* refers to your inner experiences, and the *"without"* represents the out-picturing of your inner reality.

This law says whatever is above (Heaven) is found below (Earth). The Lord's Prayer speaks of *"...on earth as it is in heaven."* Therefore, if God is above in heaven, then God is also below on Earth, as you. If you are the image and likeness of God on Earth, there is an aspect of your image and likeness in heaven. You are not a small creature. You are a big soul created by God for god-like miracles like subduing the earth and having dominion over it.

You were not given life to work hard and die. That is called slavery. You are here to live your best life and have as many god-like experiences as possible. You are here to be free, happy, and healthy. Is God in heaven sick? No! So, how can you be of God who is in heaven and be of God sick on earth? If there is no sickness in heaven, there should be no sickness on earth. If there is no lack in heaven, by law, there is no lack on earth. The significant part is, if you exist on earth, you also exist in heaven, plain and simple!

The Law of Vibration

The Law of Vibration is the third immutable Universal Law.

It states nothing rest. Everything moves. Everything is in constant flux. Everything vibrates, either positive or negative. Like energy attracts like energy. Many confuse this law with the *law of attraction* (not a law in Hermetic teaching or mine). There is a critical distinction between attraction and vibration.

The *law of attraction* posits manifestation occurs when you draw an object *to you* from the external. So, if you want a new car, you laser focus on the vehicle, you think about how you will feel driving the car, you find a picture of the car, you put it on a vision board, etc. Eventually, you will get the car because your focus was drawing it to you. Whereas, the Law of Vibration states it is your inner vibration that resonates with the things coming into your life. The attraction happens from the inside out, not the outside in.

Therefore, your inner vibrational tone is what is attracting everything to you. You have to become the vibratory match for the thing you intend to attract. Instead of calling the thing to you from the external, you shift your consciousness internally to the Kingdom of God, or the *"I already have it"* vibration. This is the distinction between vibration matching and attraction. For example, if you feel abundant within your consciousness, you are likely to attract abundance in your outer experience. If you are a miserable person on the inside, most likely, you will attract other miserable people and situations to your life. If you desire to change your life, you must raise your vibration to be the vibratory match to the things you truly wish for in your life.

The Law of Polarity

The Law of Polarity is the fourth universal law and the first mutable law. This law tells us everything exists in duality on a polarity. For example, hot and cold is the same thing—temperature, but at different degrees or two different sides of the pole (see Figure 4). This law is considered mutable because you can choose which side of the polarity you wish to vibrate. You do so by transforming your fear-based thoughts to thoughts of love. How? By changing your negative thoughts to positive thoughts by raising your vibration and choosing to stay on the positive end of the pole.

When you are experiencing difficulties on the job, you can choose to stay on the positive side of the polarity and reap the benefits of positive vibrations or choose to respond negatively and suffer the negative consequence of the energy on that side of the pole. It is your choice. This law lets you know you always have a choice; it is called *free will.*

Figure 4: Temperature Polarity

TEMPERATURE

TOO COLD--------------- | ------ | ----------------**TOO HOT**

PERFECT FOR ME

You become a victim of negativity when you do not understand how to move along the pole from the negative side to the positive side and stay there. You have to learn how to master your energy to find the perfect balance for yourself. You are in control of your energy no one else is, period!

The Law of Rhythm

The law of rhythm is the fifth universal law and the second

mutable law. This law lets you know everything has a flow-in and out, waxing and waning, ebbing and flowing—the pendulum swings in both directions-back and forth. Nothing stays the same. There is a cycle and season for everything in life. There is a rhythm or a *flow*. You will know when you are operating within this flow when things are moving along effortlessly. If you are experiencing a situation where nothing seems to be working out, and you always feel like you are going uphill, this might indicate you are not operating in the natural flow of things. Operate within the natural flow of the work environment and observe the difference. Study the rhythm of the workday, month, and year. When is the high season, and when is the lull?

Stay in the flow of things, especially on the job. You know your co-workers who are hopeless contrarians. They always have something contrary to say, especially when all others have reached a consensus. They are not operating in the flow of things. Do NOT be the contrarian on the job. Try to flow with the rhythm of the work environment. Being in the *flow* can reduce stress. Put it to the test. Go with the flow. See what happens.

The Law of Cause and Effect

The Law of Cause and Effect is the sixth Universal Law and the third mutable law. The Law of Cause and Effect says every *effect* has a *cause*. If there is an effect, there must have been a cause. Based on this law, your inner mental world is the *cause* and everything in your outside physical world is the *effect*. This law lets you know there is nothing called chance or luck. Everything in your life is *caused*. Your mind is the *cause*, and your life is the *effect*. You can create your external world by becoming more intentional—being the *cause* of your *effects* or outcomes.

If you take some time to reflect on this law, you will understand how you are causing everything to come into your life by the thoughts you harbor in your mind. If you change your thoughts, you will change your life. You are in control. End the blame game and take 100% responsibility for your thoughts and actions.

Those who understand the biblical principle of reaping and sowing, can understand the Law of Cause and Effect and can apply it to the workplace. It is the same. Understanding this law allows you to know what you are dealing with on your job on a day-to-day basis has everything to do with what you are sowing into the situation. Are you sowing peace, cooperation, love, and kindness? Or are you sowing something else? The Law of Cause and Effect says that whatever you give out, you will get right back with precision. So, if you are dealing with foolishness on the job, you are most likely engaged in the folly first. Check yourself before you point fingers. The Law of Cause and Effect also assures you that if you are being persecuted on the job, it is probably because you are holding guilt for being a persecutor in a previous situation or previous incarnation. These negative experiences are a call for you to clean up your energetic field. Start being the *cause* of what you want in your life and stop being blindsided by your *effects*. They are yours and no one else.

The Law of Gender

The last of the seven Universal Laws, and last mutable law, is the Law of Gender. The Law of Gender lets you know everything in nature has a masculine and feminine component, and both exist in the plant and animal kingdom. Yes, both males and females are needed for creation, so when I say, "males and females," I am speaking energetically, not only physically. Both feminine and masculine energy exist—Yin and Yang, for example. Even among emotions, there are feminine qualities and masculine. This is not to say females are one way, and males are another. This is about masculine and feminine energy, not bodies. Some people anchor feminine energy but are encased in a male body and vice versa.

The Law of Gender says both components exist within you. You choose how to express yourself in each incarnation. As a human being, you hold the power to express both masculine and feminine energy. It is up to you to recognize when to use each type of energy strategically and for your highest good. Dr. Fuqua says you may think you are female (or male) in this incarnation, but just wait! You may be the opposite gender energy in a future incarnation.

9 CHAPTER 9

GOD AND DNA

The universe leaves insightful clues about your divine identity. I called these clues *"universal breadcrumbs"* because if you follow them, they lead you to a deeper understanding of your divine identity. Universal breadcrumbs are hidden in your name, your birth date, birth city, in the palm of your hand, and just about anywhere you look, as long as you are looking. For me, I always wondered why my initials were DNA (Denise Nafeeza Asia), So I decided to find out why.

In 2013, I found an offer from *Groupon* for a DNA ancestry test. I purchased it and followed the directions. I mailed in the kit and waited for my test results. Upon receiving my results, I immediately went into an existential crisis. I disagreed 100% with the results, so I called the lab to let them know they had made a mistake.

According to the results (see Figure 4), I was 54% Caucasian, 38% sub-Saharan African, and 8% East Asian. I understood the East Asian part because I watched a documentary on Genghis Khan whose claim to fame was spreading his genetic material among so many women that scientists believe many can trace their ancestry back to him. I was cool with East Asian, but I did not understand the Caucasian result. I know I have some Spanish heritage from my maternal great-grandmother, but certainly not enough to produce a result of 54% Caucasian. I even called my parents and asked them if there were any White people in my family line that I should know about. They did not. My mother is of African descent, mixed with a touch Amerindian, South American indigenous Indian. My father is an Indian descendant born in Guyana, South America, with no mixture. I called my cousin, Shah Gibson who is the family genealogist and asked him about my results. He told me some genetic testing companies combine genetic data from Europe and India on one map and call it Europe. This explanation was plausible. I am not Caucasian; I am 54% Asian Indian.

Figure 4: DNA Bacchus Ancestry

Biological Ancestry Results

ESTIMATES	ANCESTRY
54%	European
38%	Sub-Saharan Africa
0%	Indigenous American
8%	East Asian

Next, I focused on my maternal DNA result. This test traced my X chromosome as far back as it would go. My maternal DNA traced back to *haplogroup L,* which is the most ancient of all human Haplogroup. This group is believed to have emerged somewhere around 170,000 years ago. Most importantly, my *haplogroup* group indicated I am a daughter of *mitochondrial Eve,* who lived over 3 million years ago! I do not know if this is exciting for you, but it was fascinating for me. I realized I am alive today because I share DNA with a woman who lived 3 million years ago. As a daughter of *mitochondrial Eve*, I had to wonder, who was her mother? And who was her mother? I am sure *mitochondrial* Eve's great-grandmother had a mother. Who was she? It came to me that if I went back far enough in this bloodline from *mitochondrial* Eve and her mother's, mother's, mother's, mother's, mother, I would eventually encounter my original DNA-or God-Self.

My initials are universal breadcrumbs that confirm my divine genetic identity—God. How absolutely delicious and exciting is it to know I am, undoubtedly a genetic replication of God. The Bible provides support for the finding of *spiritual* reproduction, as stated below:

> *"The Spirit itself beareth witness with our spirit, that we are the children of God." (Romans 8:16)*

God created us as His children and through this divine union we are, according to 2 Peter 1:4,

> *"….partakers of the divine nature."*

Who am I?

I *Googled* the meaning of my name. According to *Google*, *Denise* means to be devoted to *Bacchus*. Denise is from the Greek god Dionysus and Bacchus is the same god in Roman mythology. This universal breadcrumb was pivotal to my spiritual path. Denise or Dionysus is associated with the Egyptian God Dionysus Osiris. Osiris, in Egyptian mythology, symbolizes your *"Higher Self."* The identity of

Dionysus Osiris, who predates Jesus, is curiously similar to the life and legend of Jesus (see Table 2).

Table 2: Identity of Dionysus

- Dionysius was born of a virgin on December 25th or the Winter solstice.
- He is the son of the heavenly Father
- As the holy child, he was placed in a cradle/ crib/manger/ among beasts.
- Dionysius was a traveling teacher who performed miracles.
- He was Vine and turned water into wine.
- Dionysius rode in a triumphal procession on an ass.
- He was a sacred king killed and eaten in a Eucharistic ritual for fecundity and purification
- He traveled into the underworld to rescue his loved ones, arising from the land of the dead after 3 days.
- On March 25th, he rose from the dead, and ascended into heaven.
- Bacchus was deemed Father, Liberator, and Savior
- Dionysius was considered the only begotten Son, King of Kings, God of Gods, Sin beater, Redeemer, Anointed One, and the Alpha and Omega.
- He was identified with the Ram or the Lamb.
- His sacrificial title Dendrites or "Young Man of the Tree" indicates He was hung on a tree or crucified.

Should I think of being named Denise N. A. Bacchus with this rich history and spiritual connectedness was given to me randomly? I do not think so. I have this name by divine design. What about my nickname—Niecey? Even my nickname is curiously connected to one of the Biblical names for God—Jehovah Nisi. In fact, Psalms 82:6 clearly tell me,

"You are gods; you are all sons of the Most High."

The clues about your identity have always been with you. Open your eyes and look around. You will be surprised at what has always been staring right back at you.

The soul always knows what to do to heal itself. The challenge is to silence the mind.—Caroline Myss

10 CHAPTER 10

THE CONTRACTS

I was introduced to the concept of sacred contracts through the work of internationally renowned speaker and teacher of human consciousness, Carolyn Myss (2007). Myss teaches spirituality and mysticism and considers herself a medical intuitive. She explains that sacred contracts are agreements made between yourself and other beings of light (in heaven/Source) before you journeyed to the earth plane. Together with each participant, you carefully outlined the purpose for your incarnation including the opportunities, challenges, obstacles, and karma you agree to release.

This contract, according to Myss, is your divine blueprint. The experiences you have on earth are designed to challenge you and push you to grow to a higher level of spiritual consciousness. These contracts also help you to learn to forgive and to experience true love.

Archetypes

Who are you? Myss suggests one method to understand who you are, at least in this incarnation is to discover your *archetypes* or the *"predefined patterns of behavior that we are each born*

with" (2007). Information about the archetypal psyche or the mindset of the character you play upon your arrival to earth is contained in your pre-birth sacred contract. She further states you will play at least eight archetypes throughout your lifetime. Four of these are typical among most humans— the *Wounded Child*, the *Victim*, the *Saboteur*, and the *Prostitute*. The *Wounded Child* always needs attention and seeks it from anywhere and everywhere. When aligned with *The Victim*, these two always feel something or somebody is doing something to them, and it hurts.

Table 3: Myss Archetypes

Addict	God	Prostitute
Advocate	Goddess	Queen
Alchemist	Guide	Where
Angel	Healer	Rescue
Artist	Wounded	Saboteur
Athlete	Healer	Samarian
Avenger	Hedonist	Scribe
Beggar	Hero/Heroine	Seeker
Bully	Judge	Servant
Child: Orphan	King	Shapeshifter
Child: Wounded	Knight	Slave
Child: Magickal	Liberator	Storyteller
Child: Nature	Lover	Student
Child Eternal Boy/Girl	Martyr	Teacher
Child: Divine	Mediator	Thief
Clown	Mentor	Trickster
Companion	Messiah	Vampire
Damsel	Midas/Miser	Victor
Destroyer	Monk	Virgin
Detective	Mother	Visionary
Dilettante	Mystic	War Warrior
Don Juan	Networker	
Engineer	Nun	
Exorcist	Pioneer	
Father	Poet	
Femme Fatale	Priest	
Gambler	Prince	

The Saboteur will destroy your efforts to get ahead and let you know you are going to fail or look like a complete fool when considering a new project or going in a different direction. *The Prostitute* will pimp out your God-given talents and skills, especially at jobs, for pay incongruent with your ability and skills. In fact, *The Prostitute* will have you out in the world looking like everything by a child of God:

> *Hey, can I send you my resume?*
> *Do you know of any job openings?*
> *Give me some money.*

The other four archetypes you will play can be identified from among the list in Table 3 above. Myss suggests your archetypes provide vital information to help you decode your behavior. Understanding your archetypes will elucidate and perhaps explain why you have a particular behavioral pattern or interaction with the other characters (archetypes) on your life's stage. For example, you may ask yourself,

> *How does knowing I have a Victim residing in my consciousness help me overcome the powerlessness I have experienced?*

As you study the characteristics of archetypes in general, you will understand their existence in your consciousness and how to manipulate them for your good. For example, the *Victim* always feels attacked. When you identify the part of you that always feels attacked or emotionally hurt by someone else, whether something occurred or not, you now have the insight to say,

> "Oh, that's my inner Victim talking…
> Let me send her some love."

You begin to understand how to work with these archetypes for your own benefit. You no longer have to be a victim, if you out the *Victim* in your consciousness.

All archetypes have valuable information for you. Your awareness of the existence of your archetypes is the first step. For example, many of you know a family member who is a *Martyr/Rescuer* archetype. This archetype is fear-driven and responds immediately to drama, especially family drama. This person is usually front and center, ready to sacrifice herself rescuing others from a situation the person probably needs to learn from. If you do not have a *Martyr/Rescuer* in your life, it might be you. If you do have one in your life, she may be part of your sacred contract to show up and rescue you from something or someone at a particular date and time. Be glad they exist!

The *Martyr/Rescuer* is going to always be there in rescue readiness mode. These are your *"ride or die"* friends and family members. The tragedy of the *Martyr/Rescuer* is they do not realize they are neglecting their own life being concerned with everyone else's life. They usually grow resentful toward the very people they rescued as they watch how those *same* people live their best lives right in front of their faces and don't give back. Because of the nature of the *Martyr/Rescuer,* they remain in perpetual fear of something terrible happening in someone else's life that they must respond to. As a result, they go nowhere significant in their own lives.

Myss states throughout numerous lifetimes you will play all the roles within your family soul group. Playing each role allows you to gain a deep understanding of your family member's *"pain perspective."* The *"pain perspective"* is the psychological standpoint that helps you develop empathy and compassion for each other when you realize that you at some point in this cosmic dance, you were the drunk or the abuser, or you were the molested child or the molesting adult. How would you understand this pain if you did not experience it yourself? Myss suggests playing all the role(s) in your family dynamic gives you a visceral understanding of each other's pain. With this insight, you can forgive and love again.

On the job, the *Victim* can show you what you need to acknowledge about yourself to end the vicious cycle of victimhood. If you are always being singled out on the job, ask yourself,

> *What is this experience trying to teach me?*
> *How do I rise up from here?*

Today's *Victims* are tomorrow's heroes. They can offer wisdom from *rock bottom*. Once they reclaim their power, they become guides to the healing path of empowerment for others. You may also ask,

> *How can archetypes help me learn about my dark side or the shadow aspects of myself?*

This understanding could help you to forgive and move on. Hopefully, you will understand the role of forgiveness and its ability to end the vicious cycle of karma.

All archetypes have aspects of both the light and dark consciousness. The goal is for you to understand how your archetypes guide you in the present moment and if they are taking you in the direction you wish to go. If so, great! If not, roll up your sleeves and get to work on yourself.

"Millions of deaths would not have happened if it weren't for the consumption of alcohol. The same can be said about millions of births." — Mokokoma Mokhonoana

11 CHAPTER 11

MY CONTRACTS MY CAST

I was raised in a middle-class abusive alcoholic family. As such, specific roles emerge in every abusive alcoholic family as they did in mine (Hinrichs, DeFife, and Westen, 2011). These are the cast of characters I agreed to do life within my abusive alcoholic family of origin:

- *The Abusive Alcoholic,* played by Father.
- *The Victim,* played by Mother.
- *The Hero* or *The Parentified Child,* played by Older Sister.
- *The Clown and Star Child,* dual roles played by 2nd Sister.
- *The Scapegoat,* played by First Brother.
- *The Lost Child/Fader,* played by Second Brother.

My father played the role of the *Abusive Alcoholic.* He was a charismatic drunk. He was usually the life of the party and boy, oh boy did he party hard with alcohol. I am sure he had his own childhood issues that led him to consider alcohol although he was raised in a Muslim home. In addition to being a heavy social drinker, he was also violent and unrepentant for his deeds. When called to accountability for the destruction his behavior caused, he blamed everything on the alcohol and moved right along. Despite his erratic behavior, I loved my father. He seemed to love me back. I loved so many things about him that were opposite to my mother. He was very tidy, orderly, impeccably dressed, and smelled good all the time. He spent more time with me and did not chase me away when I had questions. He supported my curiosity by buying me any book I wanted. He showed me the softer side of the *Abusive Alcoholic.* The side that requires love and forgiveness after the violence.

This character showed me the out-picturing of *violent self-abuse.* It taught me I was energetically being violent towards myself. It showed me what deep self-hatred and self-abuse looked like. Although I felt good about myself, subconsciously, I am abusive to myself. This self-abuse is apparent when I am not making the best choices for my physical self or my spiritual growth and development.

The Victim, played by my mother, showed me what victimhood looked like. Playing the Victim is not pretty. It looked pathetic to me. I always had a lack of compassion for my mother because I felt she could have done more to stand up for herself. It looked like she chose to be a victim every time she went back to the violence without making sufficient demands for behavioral change. She exposed her children to her violent marital relationship and created the path for her daughters to subsequently end up in violent relationships.

Later in life, when the tables turned and I played the role of *The Victim* in my abusive relationship too. I learned partner violence is psychologically paralyzing. There is only so much *The Victim* perceives she can do. I discovered *The Victim* makes the best choices she can at the moment. It may not be the popular choice, however, because the choices are being made out of fear, not love. Nonetheless, I learned to develop compassion for my mother and myself. This is how I learned the pain perspective of the Victim, by playing this role as well.

The Hero or *The Parentified Child's* role was to pick up the pieces, clean up the mess, and keep the home functioning while *The Abusive Alcoholic* and *The Victim* recovered from their violent episodes. After a brutal attack, I watched *The Parentified Child* take command of *The Victim's* parental responsibilities while The *Victim* was busy recovering from her injuries and trying to hide the physical evidence so she could go back to work and act as if nothing happened. *The Parentified Child* ran the house. She cooked, paid the bills, organized chores, and tried to shield us from the reality of our violent family. She was a fixer. She fixed everything so the family could continue to function. She learned this role oh, so well that even in her adult life she cannot see how the *Parentified Child*, not her true Self is currently running her life in her own well- documented abusive marriage. She has chosen to pass the tragedy of family violence on to her own children.

My brother, the third born, was *The Scapegoat*, also known as *The Problem Child*. His role was to divert attention from the real problem—alcoholism and violence. As long as *The Scapegoat* was acting out, *The Abusive Alcoholic* and *The Victim* could point to him as the root cause of the family problems. He was the problem, not *The Abusive Alcoholic's* violence. *The Problem Child* ran away from home, had brushes with the law, was rebellious, and in high school, he was always in trouble. The one thing my parents agreed about was something had to be done about *The Problem Child*.

This took the focus off of their problems and transferred it to his acting out behavior.

My youngest brother played *The Lost Child or The Fader*. This is the child who operates under the radar. He fades into the background. He gives no trouble, and he does nothing significant to draw attention to himself. *The Lost Child/Fader* is an emotional drifter. He is quiet, invisible, and disappears to his room, often with his own alcohol supply. His goal is to live his life causing no trouble thus, drawing no attention to himself. The tragedy of *The Lost Child* is he is a metaphor for the family's dysfunction. He keeps the family secrets. He hides skeletons in the closet. He will never out the family for the proverbial *"elephants in the room."* He believes his issues do not matter and stay fading in the background of the family problems. He learns to hide his emotions as an adaptation to family dysfunction.

As for me, I played the dual role of *The Clown* and *The Star Child*. As *The Clown*, my part was to bring levity back to the family after a violent episode. Everyone counted on *The Clown to* make *The Abusive Alcoholic* happy again or laugh in order to lift the emotional tension in the home. *The Clown* distracted *The Abusive Alcoholic* with stellar report cards, academic and athletic awards, jokes, jigs and anything that would change the emotional climate in the home. *The Victim* would use *The Clown* to communicate with The *Abusive Alcoholic*. This emotional tug-o-war always put *The Clown* at the center of the family drama often feeling the need to do something for them and not focusing on herself.

The flip side of *The Clown* is *The Wounded Child*. In this context, *The Wounded Child* feels intense sublimated emotional pain and is angry. She feels trapped in an unpleasant situation where she perceives no control. *The Clown* goes about life with a large smile and large personality, yet is so wounded on the inside that this drama is predicted to play out on the job and in all her intimate relationships. She always seems caught up in the middle of the drama and never understands how she got there.

As *The Star Child*, I was the one winning all the awards at school and in sports. As long as *The Star Child* was performing well academically, *The Abusive Alcoholic* and *The Victim* could point to *her* success and feel *they* were not so bad. After all, despite all their dysfunction, they produced a Ph.D. with all the bells and whistles. *The Star Child* is always under pressure to perform and is very insecure. She is always seeking external validation. In my case, the Star Child excelled academically; yet emotionally she was a train wreck. She was always sad, never happy. Never satisfied. Never felt good within her being. Never felt ok.

Unbeknownst to me, these characters and events were part of the sacred contracts I made with this soul group to teach me ALL my spiritual lessons. Theoretically, this was the way I agreed to learn my soul lessons and these characters made similar agreements to assist me in my process. Therefore, there are NO mistakes and NOTHING to forgive. I must take 100% responsibility for the lessons I came here to learn: learn to love, accept myself, learn to forgive, heal my mind.

You have to grow from the inside out. None can teach you; none can make you spiritual. There is no other teacher but your own soul."
—*Swami Vivekananda*

12 CHAPTER 12

MY SOUL'S JOURNEY

Professional Black women who consider themselves more spiritual than religious strive to understand their spiritual selves within the microcosm (self) and the macrocosm (the Universe). They understand concepts like *sacred contracts,* the *soul's journey*, and *mastering energy*. They study Universal Law and its application to their lives. Despite all my college degrees, I was never exposed to this information, nor did I understand my relationship to the spiritual realm.

Typically, a soul's journey begins after experiencing a protracted period of discontent, significant pain, and maybe a considerable measure of suffering. When I recognized I was on my soul's journey, I was well into my career as a university professor. I already had my share of pain and suffering, both personally and professionally. Academia is stressful in general and is more stressful for women, and even more stressful for women of color. However, the way my vibration was set up guaranteed I would experience drama anywhere I went.

In 2009, my contract with my employer ended. I was happy because I encountered more than my share of *"ism"* I could stand. The attacks were many, as were my complaints. In the end, the status quo prevailed, and I was on the job market. Again.

After several grueling campus interviews, I was extended an academic appointment at an HBCU—historically Black College/University. I was elated because I felt I would not encounter any of the problems of discrimination and lack of cultural competence I experienced at the previous PWI—predominantly white university. In fact, I so wanted to call this new assignment my last assignment. I felt I could be safe among the university's unique diversity. Well, I was in for a very rude awakening.

From my very first encounter, issues of my racial and ethnic identity were questioned. The Chair of the social work department remarked upon meeting me for the first time me,

You are not Black!

My immediate thought was,

Oh, no! Not this again!

Not another so-called educated person, questioning my ethnicity and my physical appearance. My first thought was,

Wow! Isn't this a human resources violation?

I needed a job in a warm climate, so I ignored the comment, went through the motions, and signed a contract with this HBCU.

I tried to be a team player. I really did. However, this female African American Chair bullied me daily. She even encouraged the other weak faculty, staff, and students to bully me too! The last straw was when she called me back to campus after the semester was over to submit a failing grade for a student she did not like. I refused to fail the student because the student met or exceeded all the requirements for graduation. Since I refused to tow this line, both the student and I became targets of the Chair's abuse and the abuse of her office which she used to hurt us.

The more I used the chain of command to lodge my grievances (PFC), the more I was placated or ignored. The faculty whom I felt would stand up for this departmental injustice kept their heads down and mouths shut. They knew what was going on, but they were not going to stand up for me. They were there to teach about *social justice* in class, but not be about it in real life.

After numerous back and forth meetings with human resources, affirmative action, the VP of Academic Affairs, the university President, and lawyers, etc., the administration sided with the Chair. No one wanted to challenge her, probably because she had dirt on them too. This is how they rolled at this HBCU—sneaky and underhanded. So, in 2013, my contract was not renewed. I had a year to find alternative employment. The Chair had also pulled the student's scholarship, forcing her to pay back almost $18,000.00 she received as a training grant. She even waged a smear campaign against the student that blocked her from the job she trained for and earned upon graduation. I felt powerless to respond. I was out of a job myself, and soon I would not have health insurance for my children or myself. My health problems, high blood pressure, hypothyroidism, gastrointestinal problems, depression, and anxiety exasperated. The root cause of the problem, I believed, was everything, and everyone was out to get me. I felt something had to change and fast, or I would die. It seemed every time I went to my doctor, I was not getting any better. The pills were not working. The doctors prescribed more pills. Months later, I was worse off, or there was no change. I began looking for natural remedies and solutions for my health issues because I knew I did not want to spend the rest of my life sick or popping pills like my mother.

Fast forward to 2016. I was in Las Vegas at the launch of a new health marketing company. I was happy because I was going to meet my business partner for the first time. I was thrilled because I had followed her on YouTube for an entire year after my job separation. She had many videos on money manifestation, magick, natural health products, and spirituality. I knew I needed all those things, so she had my full attention. In one of her videos, she beckoned to the audience to meet her in Vegas for the corporate launch. I booked tickets, and I was off to Vegas, baby!

Late one night, after the conference activities were complete for the day, I was in a hotel room with about ten women and my business partner. We were sharing and getting to know one another. Things are going great until one of the ladies looked at me and asked me a simple question,

Who are you, Dr. Denise?

The room got quiet. All eyes were on me. I scanned my brain, and I could not formulate an answer to this woman's question. Pictures started running through my head of who I believed myself to be—*mother, daughter, sister, cousin, friend, college professor, auntie*, etc. I knew I could not give any of those responses as an answer. They sounded stupid to me in my head, so it made no sense to say any of those labels out loud. I knew I was not a label or title or relationship status. That is not who I am. So instead of saying something, I said nothing. Truthfully, I said I didn't know.

In life, opportunities for introspection present themselves to push you to discover who you really are. This was my opportunity. My natural inclination was to look around and outside of myself for the answer. It was not there. Who I am is an inside job. I had to be willing to go within myself to find the answers.

But how?

I did not have that type of relationship with myself. My goal was to find out for myself an answer to the question,

Who are you, Dr. Denise?

My conscious spiritual journey began in a hotel room in Las Vegas, Nevada, of all places on earth! Over the next few months, I repeatedly asked myself this question as I stripped away the labels and beliefs, I had formed about myself, beginning with my early childhood experiences. If life provides opportunities for self-discovery, then this was it for me. I had to start unraveling the events leading up to this moment, beginning with my creation story.

My Creation Story

During one of my coaching sessions, I was asked to complete an exercise related to my *0 to age 7-birth story*. I was asked to determine the conditions and/or circumstances around my conception and birth.

> *Was I planned?*
> *Was I wanted?*
> *Who raised me?*
> *Were there adequate resources in the household where I was being raised?*

Well, to answer those questions, I had to seek out my mother. She had this information. Her responses would have shaken me to my core if I did not already know most of this story. Basically, I was told I was unwanted and unplanned. My parents were not happy and were not in love when I was conceived.

My mother told me the story of my father brutally attacking her when she was just two months pregnant. According to this *"what had happened story,"* my parents were invited to an engagement party for one of my mother's cousins. True to form, my father was out drinking. He never showed up to accompany my mother. She rode with her aunt to the event without him. Upon her return, my father confronted her about attending the party without him. He became belligerent and attacked her.

My mother described the horrific details of my father beating her, slapping her, and hitting her with a broomstick. A family member rushed to save her (and me). My mother was hospitalized for her injuries. She was hemorrhaging from his kick to her abdomen. Upon returning from the hospital, my mother said my father never apologized or asked how she was doing. He blamed his actions on the alcohol and kept it pushing as if nothing happened. My mother still maintains my father has NEVER apologized for any of his brutality towards her or me or anyone his violence affected. As a result, I grew up to be a very angry child with a thick emotional wall and a broken heart.

My Archetypes

The Wounded Child

My first archetype, The *Wounded Child*, developed in utero. My *Wounded Child* archetype's function was to hold on to all the horrific memories of my childhood abuse, neglect, and all other childhood trauma. The *Wounded Child* was there to remind me of what everyone "*had done to me*" and keep me in a place of unforgiveness, anger, and hate. The natural predilection of my *Wounded Child* was to assign fault and blame my parents and anyone who hurt me. I found the activity of this *Wounded Child* at the core of all my dysfunctional interpersonal and intimate relationships. This child would not allow me to accept responsibility for any malicious thing I did in these relationships. She always reminded me *I* was *The Victim*, and *I* needed to be vindicated or saved.

According to the concept of sacred contracts, the higher purpose of my *Wounded Child* is to provide a path or means for me to learn forgiveness and release negative karma through forgiveness. Easier said than done! What I am aware of now is the sacred contract I made with my parents to master forgiveness. Why? Because the ability to forgive is truly divine. Forgiveness equals freedom. Although I had experienced those events, my fearful ego created an entire embellished, emotionally charged story of *"what had happened."* It reminded me I was the victim every time I felt the slightest violation of my personhood.

The story continued when I was two years old. My mother abandoned my siblings and me to immigrate to the United States. According to her story, she was making this sacrifice for our safety and future economic stability. Although she was a nurse before she married and had any of us, she could not make ends meet on her salary in Guyana. My father, who had the means to take care of us more than adequately, was irresponsible and frequently drunk. He was not a financially responsible partner to my mother or the family. With this in mind, my mother left all three of her tiny children to live in poverty with her mother and grandmother, in a rural, muddy little village in a developing nation.

From the age of two to almost six, my grandmother was my primary caretaker. I lived in a house with 10-12 people, where I was exposed to physical abuse and neglect. I do not remember seeing a medical doctor until I immigrated to the United States. Thankfully, my grandmother healed all my medical concerns with natural remedies and bush medicine. In the larger scheme of things, I had agreed to have these experiences. They had to happen, so I could be exposed to the practice of plant medicine and understand the benefits of this healing practice at a young age. This knowledge became the foundation of my spiritual healing practice.

The Dependent/Needy Child
I LOVE, LOVE, LOVED my grandmother. Granny was my

rock, my anchor, my only hope for happiness and survival. She was my protector, my comforter, and my everything. Granny always made sure I felt loved. She gave me the attention I craved. Granny made me feel safe. The more care and attention I demanded, the more she gave. Alas, *The Dependent/Needy Child* archetype emerged. According to Myss (2001), the characteristics of the *Dependent/Needy Child* carries a profound internal feeling that nothing is ever enough. The *Dependent/Needy Child* is always seeking to replace or resurrect something believed to be lost in childhood. For me, it was the love and protection of my grandmother. Coupled with *The Wounded Child*, the *Dependent/Needy Child* sets out on a life path, usually leading to pain, severe depression, and profound disappointments. Because *The Dependent/Needy Child* is so caught up in her subconscious pain, she presents as self-absorbed or focused only on her own wounds, often incapable of seeing others' needs.

Many years ago, a college mate brought this revelation to my attention in conversation when she called me self-absorbed. *Me? Self-absorbed?* I was offended. This is the normal reaction of the *Wounded Child*—always *The Victim*. I realized those who were more conscious of the dynamic of the *Dependent/Needy Child* understood me. The others judged me.

I was a spoiled brat. Spoiled rotten. Insatiable. Jealous. Mean. Nothing ever pleased my *Dependent/Needy Child,* nothing!

The Victim

At age five, two months before my sixth birthday, my mother showed up suddenly to reunite the family in New York. My parents were strangers to us. My siblings and I had not seen them in years. My first conscious memory of living with both of my parents was in the United States. We soon found out that my parents were entangled in a very physically and emotionally abusive relationship. My father was excessively abusive towards my mother and younger brother. In fact, my brother was brutally beaten for almost anything. Homework with my father was a nightmare. He would yell and scream at us even though he knew we had just immigrated to the United States. We were perplexed about the culture, the American accent, the school, and also living with parents we barely knew. We were very stressed out and traumatized children with no emotional support.

We were being raised in the U.S. according to the very formal British West Indian standards my parents inherited from the colonizers. We were expected to be disciplined—seen and not heard. We were to comply with all our parents' changing demands and requests to avoid punishment. At six years old, I decided I would never need help, especially homework help from my father. I had to avoid his brutality. I did not want to be beaten so I began to study hard and do well academically. I benefited from beginning school on the British educational system, so American academics were a breeze.

Growing up seeing my mother unconscious on the floor with the house in shambles made it easy for my wounded destructive ego to pick up with my own abusers. *The Victim* emerged right on schedule as part of the sacred contract I made for my intimate relationships. I was *The Victim* in all my relationships, and they were the victimizers. My inner *Victim* allowed me to:

1. believe everything negative that happened in the relationship was happening *to me*;

2. blame others for the circumstances of my life;

3. spend too much time in the depths of self-pity;

4. envy others who always seem to get what they want out of life;

5. feel victimized by others when situations did not work out the way I wanted;

6. stay in employment situations that did not affirm me talents and skills; and

7. allowed me to feel more powerless and less powerful.

The Law of Correspondence states my inner world is reflected in my outer world. Therefore no one could hurt me or call me ugly, stupid, or fake if I did not feel that way about myself first. Furthermore, Myss would agree the experience of victimization is the *effect* and holding guilt in my subconscious mind for being a victimizer in a previous incarnation is the *cause*. By the Law of Cause and Effect, I played the role of *The Abusive Alcoholic* father. I was the one inflicting pain on members of my cast of characters. *The Victim* popping up in my life provided me with the opportunity to recognize my role in my own victimization— I held a belief incongruent with my divine identity. By taking 100% responsibility for my error in thought, I created a path to self-forgiveness.

The *Victor* or *The Overcomer* emerged when I stopped playing the role of *The Victim* and identifying with the narrative of the ego. When I began to embrace the qualities of *The Victor*, the one whose focus is salvation, I learned the tools of forgiveness. When I learn how to love me as evidence of the out-picturing of my life, I am a witness to my spiritual growth.

"Seek not to change the world but choose to change your mind about the world."
— *A Course In Miracles*

13 CHAPTER 13

WORKPLACE VOODOO

If you skipped all the previous chapters to read this chapter, please STOP right now. Go back to where you left off and resume reading. Before you can get into this deliciousness of <u>Workplace Voodoo</u>, all of us need to be on the same page. Therefore, you have to read ALL the same pages. Please, and thank you. If you arrived at this chapter after having read **all** previous chapters, you are ready to continue. Let's go!

What is *Workplace Voodoo*? Is it using magic powers to get special treatment from your boss? Is it casting spells to get your boss or a co-worker fired? Is it cursing people with bad luck? Is it mixing up magic potions to win favor over a rival colleague?

Harmless Retaliation

Canadian scientists Bell, Rajenan, and Theiler (2012) defined *workplace voodoo* as an opportunity for *"harmless retaliation."* Full-time male and female employees (N=200) were asked to recall a problematic situation (on the job) when they felt mistreated or harmed somehow. Subjects were given *voodoo dolls* and a variety of torture options to punish the doll as if it were the offending party. The researchers reported subjects performing all types of torture on the doll (e.g., sticking the doll with pins, burning it with a candle, or pinching it with pliers). After terrorizing the voodoo dolls, study participants completed a written questionnaire. These researchers found participants who tortured the dolls reported feeling less angry and scored lower on the workplace stress questionnaire. These scientists concluded the voodoo *dolls* gave subjects a means for *"harmless retaliation"* in response to work-related stressors. So, is science now saying when you are having problems on the job, do not get mad, get a *voodoo doll*???

Hopefully, if you read all the previous chapters, you can see right through the folly of this thinking. First of all, there is no such thing as *harmless retaliation*. It may be hazardous to tap into the spiritual realm unprepared, especially with malicious intent. Instead, it would make more sense to do the self-development necessary to decode the out-picturing of the vibration (e.g. high/low) of the subconscious mind.

Workplace Voodoo is the *magick* you bring to the work environment to transform the stressful workplace into a positive energy vortex and beacon of light for yourself and others. It is recognizing *you* are *the* magickal instrument. It is the knowledge that you have the power to repel negative energy and release positive vibrations into the atmosphere. You can shift energy by moving from a low vibration to a higher vibration. The chapters on spirituality framework, levels of consciousness, and Universal Law demonstrates the mindset necessary to work problem-free on your job without the need for a *voodoo doll*. Knowing your spiritual selfcalibrates your mind to a spiritual setting where you only make the best choices that lead to the best results. You were created way before jobs were created. God created you to have life and life more abundantly. You translated this into getting a job and trading your energy for cash. Only when you achieve a higher level of consciousness will you see clearly how jobs are traps for the human spirit. This is when you realize your soul desires freedom. You seek it with all earnestness.

Fear vs. Love

Review the fear/love polarity mentioned in Chapter 3 showing the energetic repository containing *fear* on one end of the pole and *love* on the other. You have free will to choose where on the pole you want to exist vibrationally. When you create from the repository of love, only love, and good fortune will come to you. If you choose to remain unaware or unenlightened about the spiritual realm, the default choice is to create out of fear. You will experience stress, anxiety, anger, pain, and suffering. This will be your default experience, even if it is not what you want. Why? Because your subconscious mind is already making most of your decisions for you out of the repository of fear.

Choosing Fear

I chose a career as a social work educator because when I looked out at my world, there was only gloom and doom. I saw problems needing to be fixed, and fires needing to be put out. I wanted to fix them all. As a quantitative social scientist, my new role required me to examine, describe, and/or explain things about the human condition related to substance abuse, mental health, and violence. Even as a professional, I chose a career that guaranteed I see a world filled with pain and suffering. Lesson 92 in A Course in Miracles (2007) teaches it is my perceived weakness that sees human pain and suffering. I was looking through the darkness of my consciousness to see the light. I was spiritually weak, and therefore, all I could see in this mental state were the problems of the world—my world.

> *It is your weakness that sees through the body's eyes, peering about in darkness to behold the likeness of itself; the small, the weak, the sickly and the dying, those in need, the helpless and afraid, the sad, the poor, the starving and the joyless. These are seen through eyes that cannot see and cannot bless.*

This lesson further explains why I was seeing what I was seeing. I could only see my world through the body's eyes of weakness and not the eyes of strength or higher consciousness. I was seeking an intervention for the painful effect of being raised in an impoverished, violent, crazy, alcoholic family. I could not see the miracle of my life or the strength within me. According to this lesson, I must see with the eyes of Christ/God-consciousness because this is where strength lies. All else is weakness.

Application of the Law

The Law of Cause and Effect demonstrates life works like a boomerang. If you are experiencing an unfair boss now, it is because you are holding guilt for being an unreasonable boss in a past life. Scan your consciousness. Where are you being unfair to the divine purpose of your *Higher Self*? Yes, a big pill to swallow. I think I choked on this truth for a moment. I can now see how the negative experiences I had on the job were lawful and designed for me to observe what was in my subconscious mind that was being called forth for healing. By law, the horrifying work situation with the Chair at the HBCU occurred because in some other lifetime or dimension, I was a horrible boss and used my authority to do awful things to faculty, staff, and students. There would be no way I would magnetize these situations to myself if they did not exist within me. My subconscious mind out-pictured a crazy boss to help me see exactly what I needed to clean up in my consciousness.

Vibrating at such a low level guaranteed me negative life experiences. I had to wrap my mind around the possibility that maybe I created all this drama in my mind and then looked outside of myself for evidence to validate this story. The Law of Mentalism says ALL is mental. The Universe is mental, and the entire Universe exists in our mind. If All is mind, all I have to do to get different results is to change my mind. Indeed, I am the only one who can change my mind. I can do so by first taking 100% responsibility for my thoughts and actions that do not serve me.

Alchemy of the Soul

Workplace Voodoo is alchemy of the soul. It is the process of changing your mind by transmuting your mental energy from negative to positive. Changing your mind allows you to explore your beliefs about who you are and why you are here. You have to be willing to entertain the thought that maybe just maybe, you did not come to earth to be an employee. Perhaps, you came to earth to heal the lost, scared wounded child inside you so you could release those negative vibrations and rise to a higher spiritual level.

Workplace Voodoo is a spiritual awakening. It begs you to elevate your consciousness to overcome *The Victim* mindset. Knowing you cannot heal your mind with the same mindset that created the problem first, you must renew your mind and choose different thoughts. Workplace Voodoo is designed to change your mind and create a path to spiritual enlightenment. The Bible encourages you to renew your mind as a prerequisite to spiritual enlightenment by being born again—in the mindset of Christ/God-consciousness or the consciousness of love, not fear. John 14:6, Jesus tells us:

I am the way, the truth, and the life.

In revealing this, the archetype of Jesus the Christ wanted you to see Him as the example of the Way to everlasting peace. Jesus the Christ teaches you how you are to think (consciousness) and how you are to live (oneness) so you can overcome third-dimensional pain and your own human need for suffering. And in doing so, you will never ever have another problem on the job again. This is the essence of Workplace Voodoo.

The greatest weapon against stress is our ability to choose one thought over another.
—William James

14 CHAPTER 14

THE RESOURCES

Professional Black women reported using several resources for coping with work-related stress. Table 4 shows the rank-ordered results from the original study (Bacchus, 2002). Of those responding to the question, *"Yes, this is a coping resource for me,"* 97% (n=196) of PBW reported *spirituality* was a resource for coping with work-related stress. Qualitative results teased out precisely what PBW considered *spiritual resources* for coping with work-related stress (Bacchus, 2003). This chapter describes the *spiritual resources* PBW reported using to cope with work-related stress. The *spiritual resources* included in this chapter represent the women's responses and are not an exhaustive list. They are the resources and practices they reported using on the job to deal directly with work-related stressors or, in this case, problem-focused coping.

African Spirituality

PBW who actively use *spirituality* as a coping resource demonstrate a connection and a willingness to return to traditional African spirituality as an expression of their authentic selves.

Table 4: List of Coping Resources
% of women who answered, *"Yes, this is a coping resource for me"*

	n	%
Spirituality	196	97
Positive thinking	194	96
Social skills	168	83
Sister friend	158	79
Money	150	74
Church	139	69
Older family member	132	65
Family member your age	127	63
Church members	118	58
Children	109	54
Mentor	84	41
Spouse	83	36
Intimate partner	72	36
Professional organizations	72	36
Support/ self-help groups	49	24
Sorority sisters	39	19
Other	25	12

The Ashanti people of Ghana use the adinkra symbol of the *"Sankofa,"* a bird with its head turned backward retrieving an egg to emphasize this point. This symbol reminds the African diaspora to look back to their roots and extract the wisdom and knowledge from the past to use in the present. As PBW moved away from the dogma of religion and delved into their spirituality, they discovered a different spiritual frame of reference, resonating with their African roots and traditional African spirituality. As with Christianity, African spirituality acknowledges God's breath as the life force in all living things. It emphasizes *oneness* between the Creator and all creation.

African spirituality is not a religion, but a method of connecting to spiritual energy. This spiritual energy requires a balance between the self, the physical world, and the spiritual world. African spirituality acknowledges and appreciates the sacredness of everyday life and integrates this into all aspects of *being*-physical, emotional, and mental.

African spiritual practices used wherever African diasporic people are found. Many of these traditional practices have been integrated with the African American experience and over time, they became the foundation of spiritual practices used by Black women in the United States. Some examples are *vodun, Palo Mayombe, Akan, Voodoo, Hoodoo, Santeria, and Obeah*. Most of these African spiritual traditions include involvement of the occult, animal sacrifices, and ancestor veneration. Other less dramatic spiritual practices include birthing and naming ceremony, rites of passage, wedding rituals and celebrations, African dress, languages, and natural hairstyles.

Ifa

The Yoruba people of Nigeria, West Africa, practice the Ifa tradition, which is an indigenous, earth-centered African spiritual tradition. Oral records documented its emergence approximately eight thousand years ago. The Odu is the body of scriptures, mysteries, and teachings of Ifa, which was revealed in ancient divination. The Ifa tradition is characterized by acknowledging the interdependence of all life. It suggests every life form and elements in nature— rivers, rocks, clouds, metals, flowers, thunder, and the wind— have an inner soul force or Ashe. These natural energies making up the Universe are called *Orisa*. Each *Orisa* has a specific function. According to this system, humans are continually communicating with *Orisa* energy, whether they are aware of it or not. Divination is the primary method to ensure an individual is in balance or alignment on the path of their life destiny.

PBW reported involvement in *Ifa* because they felt it offered a means for connecting with ancestor spirits, spirit guides, and *Oludumare* (the supreme God). Once connected, they tend to maintain these relationships throughout the rest of their life. Currently, more Black women are seeking to join with their *spiritual court* because they believe their ancestors and spirit guides are present with them and are willing to help them. Black women learned how to interact with these entities to receive messages, warnings, information, and guidance. A recent online article indicated Black women, especially millennials, are practicing Yoruba spirituality as an alternative to the Christian practices passed down from their parents (Samuel, 2018). The author cites a quote from the interview,

> *The Church is oppressive for a lot of black women, said a 32-year-old government program analyst.*

> *But these African traditions empower*

women. They're empowering you to have
a hand in what you're doing—to create
your own magic.

Typically, traditional African spirituality includes building altars, burning sage and incense to clear negative energy, lighting candles, making food offerings, wearing specific colors or garb, and for some, animal sacrifices. Practitioners also use divination for answers or counsel for earthly things like romantic pursuits, professional advancement, relieving stress, protection, and banishing negativity. Many women practice their spirituality openly. However, a growing number of these women practice in private. They prefer the safety of meeting in online communities. They also prefer purchasing spiritual supplies online to avoid public attention. Most still fear the negative responses from their Christian families, friends, and especially people on the job. PBW, who are more advanced in their practice, typically care less about what others think about them or what they do. These women have realized that as long as they are judging themselves, they will attract people who will judge them as well. Instead, highly spiritual women tend to attract a community of people who love and support them on their spiritual journey.

Altars

An altar is a place of focused spiritual attention. It is the landing place for your spiritual activity and is a means of connecting the physical world to the spiritual. Whether you know it or not, you make altars all the time. At work, your desk is your altar. Sentimental objects are placed on your desk for your enjoyment. This is the basic concept of an altar—providing a place for your spiritual implements and space for you to connect with your ancestors and spirit guides. It is also a place you go to find joy, peace, and satisfaction.

Desk Altars

Although it was never my intention to make my work desk an altar, I recall setting it up like it was an altar. I put an Ashanti Kinte cloth across my desk and strategically placed photos and other sentimental tchotchkes on the desk altar cloth. I had gifts from students, colleagues, art from my children, things I acquired traveling, and free stuff from campus. Of course, I had my computer, printer, and all the things I felt brought me peace and happiness. I printed out positive affirmations and taped them around my office to clear my mind of negativity. I always had a Bible and other inspirational readings on or in my desk. I had my poems, a Star of David, and a crystal cross. I am not sure why I put all those things there. What I do remember is feeling drawn to these items and feeling compelled to display them somewhere. Since I spent so much time at work, these items brought me peace while I was there.

Professional Black women who identify as *more spiritual* reported being very intentional about setting up altars at work. If you know what to look for, you may notice these altars. Some have religious artifacts, candles, water, bells, crystals and stones, various colors, mirrors, fans, plants, written spells, affirmations, motivational sayings, psalms, proverbs, and more.

At home, you can erect all kinds of altars. There are ancestor altars, wealth altars, angel altars, sacred altars, candle altars, meditation altars, and special occasion altars. Your home altars may be more elaborate than the work altars for reasons of convenience or privacy. These altars are used to call in specific spiritual energies and are a constant reminder of your spiritual path. Although almost anything can be an altar, authentic altars are made of natural materials like wood, glass, or stone. Usually, there are four elements (earth, air, fire, and water) represented on every altar. There are deity altars dedicated to working with specific entities that require particular items on their altar. Customarily, the individual will receive instructions through dreams or in meditation on what to put on the altar. There is no wrong way to set up an altar if you are careful to follow instructions from your spirit guides.

Angel Contact, Angel Consciousness, Angel Work

Angel contact, angel consciousness, and angel work is communication with angels for purposes of spiritual assistance, developing altered states of consciousness, engaging psychic powers, and forgiveness work. Working with angels is not new. The Bible and other holy books are replete with examples of angel contact in various settings and situations. Angel speak, or angel talk, is an emerging spiritual practice that helps you connect with your divine nature, the microcosmos (self) with the macrocosms, (the universe) to receive messages from angels. The Bible suggests God loves you so much He created angels to protect, guard, and guide you from the time you were born to the time of your transition from the earth. Angels appear to you in various stages of your life. Babies are said to be in constant communication with their angels.

Although you may not see your angels, they are ever-present, and they are here to assist in your time of need. Angels are intermediaries between you and God. They are assigned to individuals, families, and territories. They safeguard households and restrain demons. They can also nurture, counsel, and heal you. PBW call upon their angels to assist any kind of work-related stress. They ask angels to help them with forgiveness, especially forgiving an ornery boss or co-worker. Angels help by surrounding the affected individual with white protective energy. They can soften the heart of the offended and help them see the situation from a higher spiritual perspective. Angels also encourage you to heal emotional wounds like disappointment, if you did not receive the promotion, so you can live in peace on the job and at home.

Types of Angel

Archangels

Archangels are guardians of people and all things physical. These angels are most commonly known because they are mentioned by name in the Bible- *Michael, Gabriel, Uriel, and Raphael.* These angels are called upon to assist with specific duties of providing direction, protection, and healing.

Cherubim

Cherubim are the keepers of celestial records. They record and hold the knowledge of God. Although it is not their primary purpose, cherubim can be called upon to reveal God's wisdom for specific situations on the job.

Dominions

Dominions of angels exist to ensure the cosmos remains in order by sending down power to heads of government and other authority figures. Zadkiel is the chief of this order. You can call upon this angel to help you with maintaining order in your workplace.

Seraphim

Seraphim are angels closest to God. The Bible indicates they encircle His throne and emit an intense, fiery light representing God's love. Their job is to adore and praise the Most High God.

Thrones

Thrones look like great glowing wheels covered with many eyes. They are known as God's chariot. They dispense His judgment and carry out His desires for us. These angels exist in a state of transition between the celestial and terrestrial worlds. They are considered heavenly governors who mediate between the physical and spirit world.

Astrology

Eastern (Chinese)

The Sheng Xiao or Chinese Zodiac is based on a twelve-year (not month) cycle. Each year in the cycle related to an animal sign. These signs are *the rat, ox, tiger, rabbit, dragon, snake, horse, sheep, monkey, rooster, dog, and pig.* The Chinese zodiac is calculated according to the Chinese lunar (not solar) calendar. Eastern philosophy notes a relationship between humans and the 12 zodiacal animals. The anthropomorphized animals represented by each year influences the character of people similar to western astrology signs. Chinese zodiac reveals your strengths, weaknesses, best relationship matches, luck, and money manifestation.

Western (Sun Signs)

Sun signs are divided into 12 segments according to the position of the sun in a constellation area. Everyone has a zodiacal sign corresponding to the location of the sun at the time of birth. There are 12 sun signs- Aries, Taurus, Gemini, Cancer, Leo, Virgo, Libra, Scorpio, Sagittarius, Capricorn,

Aquarius, and Pisces. Individuals use information from their zodiac signs to detect resonance with its characteristics, predilections, and alignment. Zodiac readings can be considered a tool for divination.

Galactic Signature (Moon Cycles)

Galactic signatures are calculated based on a 13-moon cycle or natural time. Unlike the Western zodiac, which is based on a 12-month cycle (artificial time). The Law of Time explains the 12-month Gregorian calendar is inaccurate based on nature. Because this is so, the mechanical 60-minute clock is also incorrect. Living according to this irregular measure of time translates into unknown effects on space and time or your positioning in the physical world.

In artificial time, time is linear and relies on the belief that the third dimension is the only dimension. This limited perception results in the knowledge that your physical reality is the only reality. By changing your relationship with time, you can change your perception of yourself and the world. For example, spiritual people understand:

- Time is NOT quantity counted, but rather quality experienced.
- Time is NOT governed by calendars and clocks.
- Time is NOT linear, but rather fractal and holographic.
- Time is NOT money.
- Time is Art.
- Time is synchronization.

Making the shift to natural time opens you up to the realm of *synchronicity*. When operating in natural time, it is a synchronicity that governs when it is time to meet or events occur, not clocks or calendars. For example, have you ever run into someone out of the blue because your mind told you to take a different route to work? Have you ever thought about seeing someone, and they just appeared like magick? This is how synchronicity works—by divine alignment and appointment. You have many divine appointments set up for you through the power of synchronicity. What is to be, will be, by divine synchronicity, not by a calendar appointment.

Bibliomancy

Bibliomancy is divination with any holy book (e.g., the Bible, IChing, the Mahabharata, and the Quran). The process involves holding the holy book in your hands, asking questions, opening the book to a random page, and pointing to a scripture. The basic premise behind bibliomancy is allowing God to speak to you through the Word. There are verses in each holy book relevant to your situation. PBW who use this technique, believe God will lead them to the right scripture for their current experience. They tap into this wisdom for various situations. They see it as a quick way to receive answers from God.

Burning or Smudging

Burning or smudging is used to purify your personal space from negative vibrations and invites light and love into your atmosphere. This practice neutralizes harmful energies with the air element. You must have an open window or passage for negative energy to exit. Smudging with smoke is usually done at home. PBW use liquid sprays to clean and clear their workspace at work. I am providing a list curated by A *Brighter*

Wild of some of the most popular burning substances below:

White Sage
Used to "wash off" negative vibes before entering sacred space and connect to ancestral spirits. Initially used in Native American traditions.

Cedar
Invokes the spirit of the cedar tree (wise, strong, and powerful). Used in rituals of protection.

Sweet Grass
Brings the blessings of Earth Mother and invites positive feminine energy into spaces. Also used to carry our prayers of thanks to the heavens.

Lavender
Burned to invite spirits of goodness, and to protect against evil. Used in many religious ceremonies and belief traditions.

Copal
Sacred sap or "blood" of this Mexican tree is burned to give thanks to the gods, especially for our natural resources.

Frankincense
Used to protect and cleanse the soul, even in death. Used in nearly every major religion on Earth. Also thought to ease depression and promote clairvoyance.

Amber
A sweet resin burned for happiness, love, and comfort in the home.

Myrrh

This tree resin is burned in an attempt to reach enlightenment. It clears debris from your energy field and opens your perception.

Sandalwood
Sandalwood is burned to increase spiritual awareness, give power to your magick/manifestations, and aids in astral traveling. It is a sacred tree in the Buddhist tradition.

Rosewood
A prized wood in India, rosewood is used to calm and soothe both the physical and emotional bodies. It holds a powerful feminine energy and heightens your intuition and compassion.

Palo Santo
Burning the wood of this mystical tree can help you stay grounded and clear, improve your creativity, and deepen your connection to Source. It is the *"holy wood"* of South America.

Dragon's Blood
Used to invite the sacred masculine, boost vitality, and give courage, especially when doing magick/manifestation.

Burning Ceremonies

Burning ceremonies are rituals used to release negativity or pain from the past. Fire, one of the five basic elements, is used as a powerful symbol of wisdom, knowledge, passion, and purification. Burning rituals help alleviate the stress and negativity of an unsatisfying job and negative thought processes. PBW use burning rituals to cleanse and let go of painful, negative situations, especially on the job. Burning rituals are also used to gain a sense of power within yourself and satisfaction knowing the "negativity" was consumed in the fire, never to return. Burning ceremonies have grown from being religious rituals to become a spiritual practice for releasing old resentments, hurt, grudges, regrets, or suffering. They may help you focus on what is most important to you.

Although burning ceremonies can be performed at any time, the timing of burning ceremonies is essential, especially during special times (e.g., moon cycles, birthdays, special events, or New Year's Eve). Burning rituals demonstrate your willingness to let go of unwanted things in your life— from negative attitudes towards co-workers and/or superiors to unhealthy relationships with persons, places, and things to have a start fresh.

Candle Meditation

Candle meditation can be used by PBW, who find it challenging to meditate. Candle meditation entails darkening the room and lighting a single candle. You stare at the candle until you reach a meditative state. Relax, breathe, and listen for guidance. This type of meditation is perfect for women who have a hard time keeping their eyes closed and sitting cross-legged on a pillow.

Candle Magick

Candle magic is a relatively new form of magick only because candles were invented in modern history. There are prerequisites for working with candles. Each decision has pros and cons and depends on personal preference and feasibility. First, you have to decide on candle type- freestanding or tapered. Second, will you use generic candles or candles that are rolled or fixed with herbs and oils? Fixed candles are melted, formed, and cooled.

Third, will you use plain or figural candles? Figural candles come with images for a particular use. They are usually more expensive. Fourth, will you use glass-encased candles or not. Glass encased candles are heavier and more difficult for transporting due to possible breakage. Fifth, will you use religious novena candles? These are used mostly by practitioners doing deity work. Lastly, there are double action candles for reversing spells. These candles are a bit more expensive and have to be monitored while burning.

Candle Color Meaning

White candles– Destruction of negative energy, peace, truth and purity.

Purple candles– Spiritual awareness, wisdom, tranquility.

Lavender Candles– Intuition, Paranormal, Peace, Healing.

Blue and Deep Blue Candles– Meditation, Healing, Forgiveness, Inspiration, Fidelity, Happiness, and opening lines of Communication.

Green Candles– Money, Fertility, Luck, Abundance, Health (not to be used when diagnosed with Cancer), Success.

Rose and Pink Colored Candles– Positive self-love, friendship, harmony, joy.

Yellow Candles–Realizing and manifesting thoughts, confidence, bringing plans into action, creativity, intelligence, mental clarity, clairvoyance.

Orange Candles–Joy, energy, education, strength attraction, and stimulation.

Red or Deep red Candles– Passion, energy, love, lust, relationships, sex, vitality, courage.

Black Candles– Protection, absorption and destruction of negative energy and also repelling negative energy from others.

Silver candle– Goddess or feminine energy, remove negativity, psychic development

Gold candle– Male energy, Solar energy, fortune, spiritual attainment.

Crystals and Stones

There are many, many crystals and stones used for various purposes. Each stone has a specific purpose and healing properties (ex. vibration). Some stones are used alone, some are combined, and others you would never combine. Science has attested to the metaphysical power of crystals and stones. These rocks store thought energy or intention similar to how cassette tapes use magnetic energy to record sound. Because we know everything in life vibrates, the vibrations of the crystals have healing potential, and when charged with positive vibes, the stones can amplify healing.

Most often, you will be drawn to a crystal or stone. When you encounter a stone for the first time, hold it in your hand and notice if you feel sensations such as hot or cold, pulsations, or calmness or tranquility. If you have a reaction of attraction to the stone, buy it right away. This stone is perfect for your healing needs. Alternatively, you can study each crystal or stone to understand its properties and whether or not this particular artifact resonates with you.

Preparing Your Stones

Some stones will be gifted to you. Before you use your stones, I suggest you clean and clear each one with prayer and/or Florida water. Place the stones on your altar until you feel they are ready to be used. During the full moons, I put my crystals and stones outside to soak up the moon's energy. This is called a moon bath. The moon energizes or charges up your crystals to make them more powerful.

When working with crystals, you should identify a specific issue or challenge you face and choose a stone accordingly. For example, fluorite is excellent for concentration and clearing mental confusion. Citrine channels the positive energy of the sun to help you manifest your dreams. Carnelian is a powerful stone that ushers in creativity and lets you let go of old ideas that no longer serve you. Black tourmaline allows you to release unwanted behavioral patterns and bad habits. It also helps to release negative energy stored in your body or within your energy field. You can use this stone for protection, especially if you are easily affected by other people's energy. Another stone for deflecting negative energy is hematite. Hematite helps to deflect others' negative moods by grounding you and reconnecting your spirit to the Earth's energy. Below is a concise list of my recommended crystals for beginners.

Amethyst
If you seek more tranquility and calm in your life, amethyst is one of the best crystals for relieving stress and bringing

balance back into your life. It also absorbs negative energy on the job.

Clear Quartz

Clear quartz is used to help you get clarity when facing a tough decision or facing a fork in the road. This stone will help you align your mind and heart so you can move forward with confidence. Use this stone when making crucial business decisions.

Moonstone

Moonstone helps balance out emotions that give you support when you feel overly emotional or out of touch with your feelings.

Rose Quartz

Rose quartz is helpful for emotional well-being because it realigns the heart chakra to magnify feelings of self-love and the unconditional love of others.

Numerology

Numbers existed before words. Everyone has a lucky number. Just like you have a favorite color, guaranteed you have a favorite number. My favorite number is seven. I just like that number. I was number seven on the line when I pledged a college sorority. Whenever I win something, it is usually connected to the lucky number seven. What's your lucky number?

Numerology for Divination

Numerology is the sacred study of the numerical value of the letters in your name and its association with the larger cosmos. Numerology is a divination tool. It looks at the relationship between numbers and your birth date and time of birth. Every number has a vibration. For example, each letter of your name corresponds to a number. The sum of that number provides details about the interrelation of numbers and its vibration. Your birth number uncovers aspects about your character, purpose in life, what motivates you, and where your hidden talents lie.

Numerology gives you calculations for your *life path* (ex. the overall traits governing you through life); *life destiny* (ex. the number describing the tasks you must achieve in this lifetime); *soul urge* (ex. your private inner cravings, likes, and dislikes); *inner dream* (ex. this number tells you how people see you when they first meet you). You can teach yourself with online resources or seek a master, like me, to prepare your numerology chart.

PBW use numerology to determine the best time to make major career and life moves. Numerology helps women decide when to invest in a new venture or when to change jobs, or when to relocate. Some report seeing repeating numbers or *master numbers* (e.g. 11, 22, 33, 44, 55, 66, 77, 88, 99). When you begin to see repeating numbers or master numbers, pay close attention. Note where you are and what you are doing. Know you are not seeing these numbers by accident. The Universe is always sending you a message. Write things down. The most common master number observed is 1111. When you see 1111, know this is a sign from the Universe. It means you are on the right track. Keep going.

Psalms

The <u>Book of Psalms</u> is a grimoire or book of magick spells. In fact, if you ask any spiritual leader, they will agree the entire Bible is too. The <u>Book of Psalms</u> is used in prayer and meditation and for both white and black magic and everything in between. Spiritual practitioners use specific Psalms and specific verses of the Psalms as spiritual resources for divine protection, direction, fortune, breaking curses, or casting them. PBW reported reciting or writing out Psalms to bring peace or protection to their lives. Engaging the power of Psalms was used when having difficulty on the job. They reported reading and meditating on Psalms gave them a sense of peace, and knowing God is the ultimate judge who brings justice to the situation. Those using Psalms usually have a particular chapter or verse that speaks to them or their situation. They say it is like a spiritual medicine prescribed just for you.

I only knew the 23rd Psalm because I learned it in Catholic school. I recited it at home on special occasions like Thanksgiving and Christmas. Later, I learned about more Psalms and what they were for-Psalm 91 for comfort and protection; Psalms 7, 27, and 31 for protection at work; and Psalms 4 and 116 to sleep when feeling anxious at night. Every Psalm that came into my life came at the right time for the right purpose. PBW prefer to use Psalms on themselves for their spiritual needs instead of using Psalms to do "*voodoo*" or put "*roots*" on someone. The Law of Cause and Effect reminds you that whatever you do to someone is coming right back to you. Be careful of your intention. Today, Psalms are found everywhere. They are on greeting cards, plaques, motivational pictures, coffee mugs, and t-shirts.

Solfeggio Tones

I love, love, love solfeggio tones! My younger cousin, who is a deeply spiritual person, introduced me to these heavenly tones. Solfeggio frequencies are composed of six tones and are known as the tones of the Universe or sacred music. The amazing thing about these tones is their ability to balance your energy and keep your body in harmony— body, mind, and soul with sound. Gregorian monks trace the origins of these tones to a John the Baptist hymn. The first six successive notes on the solfeggio scale correlate with the first syllable of the first six lines of this hymn. These tones, when chanted, are known to bestow spiritual blessings to the individual and the world.

Table 5 below shows the frequency of each tone and its purpose. If you add the Hz of each Solfeggio tone, they sum to 3, 6, or 9. These numbers are the fundamental vibrations of the Solfeggio frequencies. The father of electromagnetic engineering, Nikola Tesla, is known for saying,

If you only knew the magnificence of the 3, 6 and 9, then you would hold a key to the universe.

Table 5: Six Solfeggio Tones

396 Hz	Liberating Guilt and Fear
417 Hz	Undoing Situations and Facilitating Change
528 Hz	Transformation and Miracles (DNA)
639 Hz	Connecting/Relationships
741 Hz	Expression and Solutions
852 Hz	Returning to Spiritual Order

From an energetic standpoint, most popular music is recorded at a tone disruptive to the human body energetic field. Solfeggio tones are so powerful, they can recalibrate your body back to a balanced resonance. PBW find these tones healing and in harmony with achieving spiritual health and well-being. PBW reported playing solfeggio tones at work to clear negative energy and increase concentration, among other benefits. These tones are used at home for spiritual healing and numerous other health benefits, even to attract money. You can locate various solfeggio meditation videos on YouTube. I have my personal favorites for relaxation and healing. You will have to listen to a few videos to find those tones matching your vibration.

Every aspect of your life is anchored energetically in your living space, so clearing clutter can completely transform your entire existence. — Karen Kingston

15 CHAPTER 15

CUBICLE CONJURING

Cubicle conjuring is engaging in spiritual practices on the job. In fact, most workers unconsciously engage in cubicle conjuring, whether they know it or not. Let's explore. There are four walls, a desk, some filing cabinets, and shelves in a traditional office environment. This environment is not meant for comfort. It is intended for completing the mundane tasks of your job description, such as cranking out reports, paper-pushing, or client services. The day-to-day activities are repetitive and individual creativity is limited. This type of environment can be suffocating to the soul. The soul's desire is God's desire—to create.

The purpose of conjuring your cubicle is to improve or shift the energy in your workspace's immediate physical environment. My apologies, you have a corner office and not a cubicle. In any event, cubicle conjuring goes beyond decorating to precisely and strategically placing objects in your workspace to improve and increase the flow of positive energy. Some workers place religious symbols/sigils, like a cross, a Star of David, the crescent and star, etc. in their personal space. These items communicate your particular religious affiliation. Other workers put up pictures of family members or inspirational quotes or famous icons. The point is, there is an innate need to *mark* one's territory with cherished items, which theoretically improves mood and brings good fortune.

For the spiritually guided PBW, cubicle conjuring is a bit more detailed and intentional. The first thing you will notice in an appropriately conjured office is order. Order is the first law of the Universe. The office space will be orderly and uncluttered. Second, you will notice the smell. A well-conjured office will smell nice. Third, you will observe interesting items, some out of the norm for the office. If you know what you are looking at, you will be able to detect evidence of cubicle conjuring. What will not be visible to you are the specific rituals and practices performed in the cubicle.

Most PBW perform these activities before or after work, out of the eyesight of coworkers. They include "*praying up*" the space reciting affirmations to fill the atmosphere with positivity. They use prayers, usually Psalms, to protect themselves and/or coworkers. These practices also repel negative energy in the form of people. In conjuring a cubicle, you can use your spiritual creativity to entertain the presence of higher spiritual beings. If you have your desk/altar set up correctly, your workday may just fly by. You begin to work, and before you realize it, it is time to be released from your daily assignment. Our enslaved ancestors sang songs to pass the time on the plantation. Cubical conjuring is similar in this regard.

Case Example

A PBW shared with me the steps she takes to set up her workspace. I will call her Janet. First and foremost, Janet keeps her workspace clean and uncluttered. This allows for the flow of good energy. She had several typed affirmations pinned up on her wall. She has a succulent to represent abundance in a blue plant pot located in the *wealth quadrant* (feng shui philosophy) on her desk. Janet said this plant represents her ability to thrive in a hostile environment. It also cleans the air and gives off oxygen. She also uses a bottle of water "*charged up*" with crystals to water her plant. The water bottle also has a piece of paper taped to it with a positive affirmation. As she waters her plant, she says the water was symbolically watering her dreams.

Next, Janet has a purple mirror, a high vibrational color to remind her everything she sees is a reflection of her subconscious mind. She has a mini fan to blow away negativity. Lastly, she had a small decorative cup containing the crystals of her choice—amethyst, clear quartz, and amber. She said these items are for generating positive energy. She switches the crystals as necessary. Because Janet cannot burn sage on the job, she routinely cleans her cubicle of negative energy with liquid sage. She sprays her workspace with a spiritual clearing concoction made with essential oils, and Florida water, or rose water. Janet also wears specially selected crystals to balance the energy around her. If necessary, she will call upon her guardian angel to protect her and her belongings while at work. She has the option to pray for her coworkers and higher-ups as well. She says praying for others is a personal decision.

The overall purpose of cubicle conjuring is to intentionally raise the vibration of your workspace, allow positive, creative energy to flow and repel any negativity. The spiritual implements used are specific to the intention; they are not trendy or just for decoration. The proof of cubical conjuring is in the experience. What do you want to experience in your workspace-heaven or hell? The choice is always yours.

The magic is inside of you. There ain't no crystal ball.
Dolly Parton

16 CHAPTER 16

THE IMPLEMENTS

The most powerful spiritual implement known to humankind is the mind. Your mind is the creative center of all your manifestations. You train your spiritual implement to do what you want them to do. If you neglect to train your mind, no matter which spiritual implement you use, you will probably make a mess! The information contained in this chapter is based on research data. It is not an exhaustive list of all available spiritual implements. Some of these implements were mentioned in the previous section as resources. This chapter expands your awareness of the repertoire of spiritual tools PBW reported using in response to experiencing work-related stress. Let's begin.

Types of Spiritual Implements

Spiritual implements are items or assistive devices used in various forms of spiritual practice. I was introduced to spiritual implements by the Catholic religion. I was exposed to things like incense, bells, rosary beads, holy water, altars, candle worship, spiritual colors, garb, holy seasons, etc. This religious exposure was an essential prerequisite for my spiritual growth. As a Catholic, I did not wholly understand the spiritual significance of these implements, nor did I question them. I recall inviting a friend to the Catholic Church with me as an adult. When the priest began walking around the church, burning frankincense in the censer, her eyes opened wide. The look on her face was priceless.

"What in the world was the priest doing burning incense in the church?"

I had no response because this was normal for me. Then there were questions about sprinkling the holy water and all the altar rituals. I did not know how to explain these rituals because they were not explained to me. I told her to be happy the service was only one hour. Typically, people are drawn to the spiritual implements needed for their particular spiritual practice. You will probably learn about different implements as you grow in your spiritual gifts. Take your time and allow everything to unfold.

Altars

Spiritual altars are specifically set up as a designated place for anchoring your spiritual energy. This is the go-to place for your daily spiritual practice of praying, meditating, or chanting. It is also the place for you to be still and hear from God. You can set up many different types of altars for many different intentions. Take your time when setting up your altar. Pay attention to your colors, placement of items, and location. You can draw inspiration from within and develop your altar. Almost all altars have a representation of the four elements: water (ex. A glass of water, air (ex. incense), fire (ex. candle), and earth (ex. a rock, wooden wand, flowers, a plant, dirt). The most important thing to remember is to stay in tune with your spirit. Your spirit will guide you and let you know if you are aligned with the purpose and intention of the altar.

Maintaining your altar is just as important as setting it up. Please do not operate from a dirty altar. You must keep your altar clean and dust-free. A clean altar shows respect for yourself, your spiritual community, and your spiritual space. I cannot emphasize this enough. I am not sure what entities you will invite or what will happen to you if you operate from an unclean altar. Service your altar daily.

Altars Cloths

Altar cloths can be plain white, any color, or multi-colored depending upon the specific intention for the altar. White is used mostly with angel and ancestor altars. The choice of altar cloth is entirely up to the individual. Allow yourself to be spiritually guided in this process. You may also elect to use an altar cloth sentimental to you or the entity you are honoring with the altar (ex. an ancestor.) I love very fancy rich-looking altar cloths, especially for my wealth altar. Try to use natural fiber like100% cotton or linen. It is all about resonance. Everything has to resonate with you and your intention for the altar.

Amulets and Azabache Bracelets

Most spiritual people are aware of both good and evil forces in their lives. They take deliberate steps to protect themselves with amulets and charms. Azabache bracelets, for example, are a type of amulet typically worn as sacred jewelry for protection from negative or evil spirits. Latinos especially believe Azabache bracelets protect against *mal de ojo, or evil eye. The Evil Eye* is the result of excessive admiration or envious looks, especially towards newborn babies. Babies and adults wear an azabache (a gold bracelet or necklace with a black or red coral charm in the form of a fist), to protect from the evil eye. Recently, I was chatting with the receptionist at my doctor's office about this book. I told her the title of my book and immediately she said she does not need any *"workplace voodoo."* I noticed she was wearing an azabache bracelet and I asked her, pointing at the bracelet,

> *What is that??*

She smiled and said,

> *This is not for protection from here...It is for something else.*

Really? So just how does this protection from evil work? Does it know when to turn on and when to turn off? I am sure she just did not want to talk about it. Spirituality is private, but spiritual implements can be observed if you know what to look for.

Ancestor Money

Ancestor money is symbolic money burned to send *money energy* to ancestors or people who have passed on. According to ancient beliefs, when your ancestors transition with debt, you and your living relatives inherit this negative debt energy. Burning ancestor money is supposed to dissolve this negative debt energy in the third dimension. In return, your ancestors will guide you, protect you, and bless you with money. Ancestor money has different names including ghost money, spirit money, Joss paper, hell/heaven notes, etc. Some ancestor money looks like play money and other notes carry the image of the Jade Emperor who is the Taoist deity ruling over ALL the money on earth.

Beads

Beads have been around for tens of thousands of years. Each religion involves beads for prayer and meditation. I learned to pray with rosary beads in Catholic School. After college, I was introduced to Buddhist prayer beads and malas. I learned how to chant mantras 108 times with beads. When I graduated with my doctorate, my mother gave me a string of white pearls, my favorite type of bead. These beads are part of my academic dress. I was given waist beads by an Ashanti friend and had been wearing them for over 15 years. I did not realize how much beads were a part of my entire life. I love beads and am attracted to gorgeous beads. I have been collecting beads because of the sentimental value of each one.

Every bead has its vibration. Each color, shape, and size is symbolic. The popular Mardis Gras beads are gold, purple, and green to symbolize Christian values of power, justice, and faith. As with all spiritual implements, allow the right beads to come to you. When you see beads that jump out at you, buy them. You may not know what to do with them first, but eventually, it will be revealed to you.

Bells, Bowls, Gongs, Horns, Whistles

Bells, more so than gongs, are very common in Western religious worship. Cymbals and tambourines are used to accentuate worship. Most churches or worship houses have bells or bell towers built into its structure. Once again, I was introduced to bells from my Catholic Church experience.

The altar boys rang bells during the communion ritual. I always wondered why, but no one ever explained it to me. Bells signal the beginning and end of worship and they usher in angels and benevolent spirits into the atmosphere. They can drive out malevolent spirits too. Sound gives a vibration that can clean and clear the atmosphere in preparation for meditation or worship—different spirits like different sounds. For example, money angels love little bells. My daughter has an Etsy shop, and she rings a bell every time she gets a notification of a sale. She does this in gratitude for the money exchange and encourages money angels to bring her more customers. You get to decide how to incorporate bells into your spiritual practice.

Bowls or singing bowls are used in eastern spiritual rituals. They are used to create a range of sounds aimed at restoring the body's typical vibratory frequencies. Sound can recalibrate the energy in the body and bring homeostasis and harmony between the body, mind, and soul. Sounds set moods and have a significant impact on how you feel during the day. I love the sound of singing bowls and the experience of calmness it brings to me. There are numerous singing bowl types. Find the ones you like the best. You may also find instructions on how to use your bowls and bowl meditations on YouTube.

Books and Holy Books

Books are an essential part of your spiritual growth and development. My Christian community insisted the Bible is the only book I would ever need to read. Although I had access to Bibles, I never really read one until I was about 25 years old. I did not know how to read a Bible, and I did not understand much of what it said. Between a lack of clarity and falling asleep after reading two verses, I always struggled to read the Bible. In 1994 when I became a born-again Christian, I dedicated myself to Bible study. I was blessed to have excellent Bible teachers who helped me understand the Bible and created a zest for diving deeper. My Bible teachers went beyond *"churchy doctrine"* to explain the symbolism and mysteries like how Jesus turned water into wine and why a mother would ask a minor child to *"hook up"* the booze for a party. I am grateful for the teaching of the Bible. By far, reading the Bible has been the most impactful on my spiritual journey. Because I did not grow up with a *churchy mind frame*, I was able to read the Bible without judgment, and this allowed the Holy Spirit/Isis to impart wisdom to me.

Holy Books Will Find You

Women growing in their spirituality probably read more than one holy book. I know I have. Like most spiritual implements, holy books usually find you. I was hospitalized for three days in the spring of 2018, when my heart rate dropped very low. I was chatting with the technician who performed my stress test. During the conversation, he suggested I read the Quran.

Although my father is a Muslim, he never introduced Islam to me as a way of life. My father felt I should choose my religion when I became of age. As such, I never read the Quran, nor did I own one. I never saw one in our home. I told the man I did not have a Quran. The next thing I knew, the man pulled out a beautiful pocket-sized Quran from somewhere and gave it to me. I almost cried when I touched it. I could feel the spiritual energy of the book. I understood the significance of receiving a holy book from a stranger.

Spirit wants to teach me something about Islam. I was going to a new level.

Aside from holy books, there are so many other books relevant to your spiritual walk. You are bound to find out how essential reading spiritual books are to your spiritual growth. Read and meditate daily. Information without revelation makes you look and sound crazy if you are just regurgitating or *"dropping knowledge"* about things that have existed for thousands of years that you are just finding out about now. Read, reflect, and let the information sink in before you start talking.

Candles

As expected, the Catholic Church introduced me to candles too. Candles are used widely in religious and spiritual practice. Type of candle, color, size all matter. The all-purpose candle color is white. So if you are not sure what color candle to light, light a white candle. Most spiritual people clean and clear their candles before use. I have a procedure I use, and I teach my clients to do the same. Overall, candles help to set the mood of your intention. Do your research or reach out for assistance with your candle work.

Cauldron

You might have seen a caldron from watching spooky TV shows of witches stirring something in a large, heavy metal pot with steam pouring out everywhere. Today, cauldrons are used in all types of spiritual practice. Cauldrons can be used to burn ancestor money, incense, sage, and paper. Ashes can be stored in a caldron and utilized for other spiritual spells and rituals. I purchased a mini cauldron this year, and I think it is so cute. I use it to save ashes from my burning ceremonies.

Cleaning and Clearing

Spiritual implements must be cleaned and cleared for use. Typical cleaning and clearing tools are various essential oils, Florida water, plain water charged with your emotional or spiritual energy, sea salt, sound (e.g., bells, chimes, solfeggio tones).

Crystals, Gems, and Stones

People have been drawn to the power of crystals, rocks, and gems for centuries. The Bible is replete with scriptural references to crystals, rocks, and precious gems (*e.g., Proverbs 3:15; 1 Chronicles 20:2; Daniel 11:38, etc.*). Even Jesus is considered the *"Rock of Ages."*

Crystals, stones, and gems have multiple spiritual uses. They can be used as the earth element on your altar. They can be used to release mental, physical, and spiritual energy blockages or imbalances in the body's energy centers (e.g., chakras). This is achieved by engaging the healing properties of stones and crystals. You have to study each stone and learn everything about their healing property and how they will be used for your spiritual growth and development. Alternatively, you can allow your spirit guides to teach you or seek out an expert.

Crystals are beautiful consciousness connectors. They help you connect to the spirit world and have the vibratory power to heal your body. The chemical compositions of quartz crystal naturally transmit energy in the form of received energy (e.g., charging up). I charge my crystals upon my altar and in the light of specific full or new moons. Charged up crystals are used as a tool to help connect your consciousness with your body for healing. Some people have an entire spiritual practice based just on crystal use. God gave us crystals for your health and healing. Use them.

Divination Tools

Professional Black women use divination to help obtain answers for questions concerning work, relationships, and decision-making. Divination tools include cards (playing, tarot, angel, color, and oracle), bones, blood, roots, mirror, water, tea leaves, and runes. These tools are used to see into your situation, bring guidance, peace, enlightenment, and help guide your actions. As with all spiritual implements, you will notice you are drawn to a particular tool(s). Be open and explore the tools you may want to work with. It takes time to develop a divination practice. Begin with yourself. Learn how to use these tools to guide your life and bring light to your situation.

Decoding Tools

The transition from the work path to the spiritual path requires continual guidance, especially from the spiritual realm. One requirement is to decode yourself. The most common decoding tools are eastern and western astrology, galactic signatures, and numerology. These tools help to remind you that from the moment your soul was birthed, an entire constellation of information about you was solidified in the universe. It is your responsibility to extract this knowledge using the decoding tool.

Decoding yourself gives you access to information to assist your spiritual journey. If you do not believe in *"this stuff,"* so mote it be. People on a spiritual path actively seek information to decode themselves. They delve deep into this study. The Bible suggests we should *seek*. In doing so, what else can you find but yourself—fearfully created by God?

Grimoires

A grimoire is a magick book. The process of creating a grimoire is to first learn how to *spell*. You learn how to spell by learning the sound of the *ABCs'*. Then you learn to combine letters, or the symbolic representation of sound, to form words. This is called *spelling*. When you learn to spell, you learn to arrange words in a particular order to create phrases and sentences using grammar. Grammar is the code to let you know if your spells have been constructed correctly. You are now capable of writing and speaking life or death into existence. You can create your own grimoire or book of spells. The process of creating grimoires and spelling is commonly used in your day-to-day life. Every text you read is using this same concept.

Advertisers know precisely how to use spells, or carefully constructed words and phrases to evoke emotions that move you to do whatever they want you to do. Billions of advertising dollars are spent to create spells aimed at transferring money from your wallet to their wallets. This practice is quite effective, as evidenced by the number of companies who have been successful in business year after year. This quote from the advertising giant, David Ogilvy, sums up his use of grammar for casting spells in advertising:

If you're trying to persuade people to do something, or buy something, it seems to me you should use their language, the language they use every day, the language in which they think. We try to write in the vernacular.

Journals

Journals and journaling are essential to your spiritual practice. Journaling allows you to take information from your subconscious and manifest it in the second dimension in the form of lines and curves on paper. It is vital to have hand-written journals and not typed. There is a difference in terms of energy and energy transfer. Once your ideas are out in the 2-dimensional world, you can observe what your mind is thinking.

Journaling is also a way to record your spiritual growth on your soul's journey. Before I write in my journal, I place it on my altar to clean and clear any negative energy it may have picked up in its production, shipping, and handling. Once cleaned and cleared, I dedicate it by writing a strong intention for its use in the front cover of the journal. After this consecration, the journal is ready to be used.

Palmistry

Palmistry or *chiromancy* is a divination and decoding practice using the palms of the hands. This is one of the only decoding tools you have at your disposal every day of your life. Some claim they can tell your future based on how the lines appear in your hands. They spend years studying and memorizing every line in the palm. They write books and create reference guides. This is the going standard of chiromancy practice. However, for me, I was born with the gift of chiromancy. I never studied palm reading. I have no idea what all the lines mean. I know for sure that I can look at the palm of your hand and see things about you and various aspects of your life that have been there since your birth.

I never thought of myself as a palm reader because I do not fortune tell, nor do I own a crystal ball. However, I recently realized I have always read palms even as a young child. Some people are attracted to various parts of the human body, I was always attracted to the palms of people's hands. I would look at someone's palm and immediately get information about their life. I kept most of this information to myself. Who would believe a child? I never appraised this spiritual gifting as a thing to be valued. Now I have learned to embrace and appreciate my spiritual gifts given to me by the All-knowing, benevolent God for His purpose, not mine. Who am I to continue minimizing my spiritual gifts? You were born with significant data in the palm of your hands. It would only behoove you to allow me to take a look.

Plants and Flowers

The plant and flower business is a multi-billion-dollar industry simply because corporations know the value of these items to elicit emotions in human beings. Every plant and flower has its own God-given characteristics. This includes its unique vibration. Each vibration has information. These characteristics and vibration of the plant or flower determine which one will be selected for raising vibration, healing, cleaning the air, and so forth. In spiritual practice, plants and flowers are used for specific purposes, whether it is creating infused water, tinctures, salves, essential oils, baths, teas, or medicine. Big pharma turns to nature to extract the medicinal properties of plants and flowers to make the next life-saving pill. Spiritual people usually cut out the middleman and go directly to nature for its cures. My spiritual healing practice entails using plant medicines (e.g., Cannabis, Ayahuasca) for healing and spiritual enlightenment.

Sigils

A sigil is a particular type of symbol. It is a symbol charged to produce an expected outcome. Sigils are used to hypnotize and mesmerize. Sigils are used in every business and industry. The *golden arches* are the universal sigil for French fries. Before my children could talk, they knew very well what the golden arches represented—French fries and fun. Nike uses the *swoosh* as its sigil to communicate *swiftness* to potential customers. Corporations like McDonald's and Nike use sigils because they understand the power sigils have on the subconscious mind to move the consumer to purchase their products. Consumers consume products they feel are aligned with an unconscious need. Most people want products aimed at increasing joy or reducing suffering.

Sigils are symbols that bend the subconscious mind in the direction of an intention. Some call this magick. In this regard, sigil magick is a means to communicate with the subconscious mind. Remember, the subconscious mind accepts EVERYTHING it is exposed to without judgment. For example, everything a baby is exposed to from the time they are born is stored in its subconscious mind. The baby does not yet have the mental capacity to discriminate between what this mind takes in and what it filters out. It accepts everything--good, bad, and otherwise. The use of sigils in spiritual practice is intended to implant specific messages via a symbol into your subconscious mind to cause your mind to produce a particular and expected result. You do not have to be a large corporation to create your own sigil. I suggest you do your own research. However, here are six steps generally accepted as a means to create a sigil:

Step 1: On a clean sheet of white paper, create a clear, active intention statement. Your statement must be positive and present tense. For example, an intention statement has words such as:

"I will" or *"It is my intention to..."*

Step 2: Convert the statement into non-duplicative consonants and delete all vowels.

Step 3: Take the phrase you wrote and convert it into a symbol. Do this by writing the remaining letters at a time, creatively connecting each consonant to each other.

When complete, you may decorate the sigil anyway you like. I would suggest keeping it simple in the beginning. Encase your sigil in a circle. This is optional. For some purposes, this is ideal. It really does not matter what the sigil looks like to others. However, it must have a deeper meaning for you. You can use a line or any geometric shape to construct the sigil. Remember, it is a symbolic representation of a truth you want to manifest in your life. So if you're going to experience love or abundance, draw a symbol, your mind would recognize easily as imbued with those qualities.

Step 4. Leave the sigil alone. This allows the symbol that was just in the unseen world to manifest undisturbed in this two-dimensional world until it is ready to be charged up.

Step 5: Charge the sigil by placing it on an appropriate altar. For example, if it is a money drawing sigil, put it on your wealth altar. You may also charge the sigil in a holy book, under a candle or glass of water. Place it in the moonlight to charge it with cosmic or spiritual energy. Some people stare at the sigil until they feel a resonance with the intention of the symbol. Repeat the charging for at least seven (7) days. Allow the sigil to absorb this energy undisturbed by worry, fear, or any negative energy.

Step 6: Once charged up, you must release the sigil into the atmosphere to do what it intended to do. You may release the sigil in a burning ritual. Burn the sigil in your cauldron. This releases it back to the Universe so it can connect with its vibratory match to deliver back to you precisely what you desired. FYI, most practitioners do not burn their sigils. Some release it in running water like a river. Others bury it in strategic places like at a bank for wealth.

Sigil magick takes time to develop. Remember to use your magick for good. Everything you do is undoubtedly going to return back to you with precision.

Wands

Most of us have seen magicians using wands on stage for magic tricks. In spiritual practice, wands are used to direct energy. They vary in size, material, and purpose. Wands are used in ceremonial magick and other methods of the occult. When you are ready for your wand, it will find you and you will know exactly what to do with it. Like the sigil, a wand must be cleaned, cleared, and charged up with your energy. You may place the wand on your altar for cleaning and clearing. You may hold your wand in your hand to recharge it with your energy before each use.

Now that you have read this chapter, I want to strongly reiterate that the most potent spiritual implement readily available to you is your own mind. Your mind is such a powerful creator. Look, without judgment, at what your mind has already created without the assistance of any spiritual awareness or implements. It is also essential for you to continually charge up your mind by feeding it spiritual food. Prayer, meditations, going into nature, and deep breathing are all forms of spiritual nourishment. Spiritually feed your mind, and you will know it is the most potent implement you could ever possess.

David built an altar to the LORD *there and sacrificed burnt offerings and fellowship offerings. Then the* LORD *answered his prayer on behalf of the land, and the plague on Israel was stopped.*
(2 Samuel 24:25)

17 CHAPTER 17

MY ALTAR EXPERIENCE

In the summer of 2017, I was inspired to set up an ancestor altar. *An ancestor altar???* That was a strange request. Why would this pop into my consciousness? I already had an altar. I had been setting up altars everywhere I go, even in hotel rooms to use in my daily spiritual practice. I also have a wealth altar for my money manifestation work. An ancestor altar was out of my league. I felt an ancestor altar was too extreme for me. It meant having contact with the deceased family members and none of my altars were geared for that.

In any event, here is my *"what had happened"* story. When I am home in the Bahamas, I usually meditate floating on my back for hours in the sea. One day, when I finished my mediation session, a thought popped in my head about setting up an ancestor altar. I did not pay it much attention until the thought popped in my head again. This happened for an entire week. I dismissed the message numerous times and I even planned to delay the set up until I returned to the United States. This was my ego's idea, of course. Because the nudging would not go away, I decided to talk about it with my spiritual community members. I told them about my experiences and that I did not know how to set up an ancestor altar. I was also confused as to why this thought would pop in my head and not go away. My spiritual sisters assured me my thoughts were not random. If I received a message about setting up an ancestor altar, I should do so right away. Obviously, my ancestors wanted to connect with me, and my job was to prepare the space.

Setting Up My Altar

I really did not know how to set up an ancestor altar. My spiritual sisters told me not to worry about how. Spirit would guide me. My job was to listen. I began receiving inspiration for what to place on the altar. However, despite the divine directions I was receiving, I decided to go on YouTube. I watched at least 20 or more "how to set up an ancestor altar" videos. Wrong move. One guy suggested writing down all my ancestor's names on a sheet of paper and placing it on the altar. He said it did not matter what kind of relationship I had with these people before they died or if the ancestors did or did not like me. It did not even matter if I knew them while they were alive. I should honor all of them on my altar. So, I did what YouTube said.

First, I covered the side table that was to become the ancestor altar with a white sheet. White altar cloths are customarily used for ancestor altars. Then I placed a representative of each element on the altar—a full glass of water (water), incense (air), white candle (fire), crystals (earth). I wrote all the names of my ancestors that I could think of on a white sheet of paper and placed it on the altar. I put all kinds of food, ribbons, a comb, nail polish, coffee, cigarettes, and alcohol. If they were my ancestors, I know they would want alcohol on the altar. I also put fresh flowers I had picked from somebody's yard on there too.

After the first 24 hours, disaster struck! I woke up to the altar being overtaken by an army of ants! Out of seemingly nowhere, a barrage of ants came marching all over the altar like they were invited. I immediately tried to get rid of the ants, but they would not go. I decided to take down the altar and clean the space again. I felt defeated. My ego had a field day with my thoughts.

"See, you should have waited until you returned to the U.S."

"You do not know what you are doing."

"You did not hear anything. You just made this up."

"Stop messing with ancestor stuff; you are starting trouble."

A day or two had passed, and I got the courage to put the altar back up. I was going to start all over again. This time, I was going to focus on my grandmother since she was the only ancestor I knew and loved. I decided to only put the things she would like and appreciate back on the altar. The next day, NO ANTS! I never saw another ant as long as the altar was up. I even placed food and drink on the altar—no ants.

The main thing I learned from this altar experience was to always listen to my inner voice. My job is to pay attention, listen, and follow the directions from my ancestors. My ancestors did not say look at YouTube videos for instructions. YouTube is a guide, not a prescription. I learned to rely on my intuition and to let my ancestors guide me through this process. If you feel called to erect a spiritual altar, I would suggest deep, prolonged meditation for clarity.

Altars send a strong message to the spiritual world that you mean serious business. This is not to be taken lightly.

Good luck!

The only person who can pull me down is myself, and
I am not going to let myself pull me anymore.— C. Joybell

18 CHAPTER 18

THE SELF-CARE

Spiritual self-care activities soothe the mind and energize the soul. Unlike self-care (day spas, girl's night out, and vacations), spiritual self-care includes extreme or unusual activities that test the limits of your endurance and humanness. Be willing to exit your comfort zone to expand your consciousness level because nothing grows in the comfort zone. Spiritual PBW know they must become uncomfortable to grow spiritually. They will do things like sit in sweat lodges; walk on hot coals or glass. They may fast for 40 days, keep silent for weeks, skydive, bungee jumping, or do something out of the ordinary just to experience. This is the extreme side of the spectrum.

Spiritual self-care is anything that brings you pleasure and connects you powerfully to your spiritual center within. You are responsible for discovering the spiritual self-care techniques best suited for your spiritual growth and development. At the less extreme end of the spectrum, spiritual self-care involves your daily spiritual practice. This chapter discusses practices you can engage in every day to charge up your soul, so this aspect of your *Self* becomes more potent than the messy ego that has been governing your life.

Prayer

Prayer must become a natural, standard, moment-to-moment behavioral practice on the spiritual path. The scripture below directs you to pray without ceasing.

Rejoice always, pray without ceasing, give thanks in all circumstances; for this is the will of God in Christ Jesus for you. (Thessalonians 5:16-18.)

This does not mean you walk around all day, mumbling or kneeling or genuflecting. Set aside time each day to engage in prayer. You pray silently throughout the day to stay connected to your spiritual source. Prayer also opens a portal for fluid communications with God and your spiritual guides. It gives you the space to ask God for what you want to manifest in your life.

Ask, and you will receive. (John 16:24).

As you see in the scripture below,

You do not have because you do not ask God. (James 4:2)

Once you have switched over to God's plan, you must know how to ask and what to ask for.

You may ask me for anything in my name, and I will do it. (John 14:14)

Through prayer, you develop a relationship with God. You can ask for anything. You know what to ask for because you are developing an authentic relationship with God. The

Universe is relational. It knows what you need and will provide it to you. Believe you have it, and it will show up for you. By developing a daily prayer practice, you get to share special time with the Creator of all things. You are praying for your own edification and not out of religious obligation. Prayer is more than just asking for something. When you discipline yourself to a daily spiritual practice of prayer, you begin to change on the inside. Your life will improve miraculously through communication with God.

Prayer Changes You

Prayer also changes the way you see yourself in your life experience. You can be a witness to all that is wonderful and delightful about your life. You begin to realize you are a walking miracle. People will notice something is quite different about you. Nothing on the outside will have the power to disturb your peace the way it could in the past. The more you pray, the more you will want to pray. Prayer is such a spiritual treat!

Meditation

Meditation is a spiritual salve for the mind. There is a part of your mind that is very crazy, loud, and destructive. You have learned this insane mind is out to get you. How? With crazy thoughts of the past or future. Some call this the *"monkey mind."* This *"monkey mind"* has rambling thoughts, jumping from topic to topic, creating so much noise in your head that you simply cannot relax. The *"monkey mind"* and all its attacking thoughts are in cahoots with your body to disrupt your peace. This crazy mind can convince your body it is sick, tired, hungry, dying, or just about any negative thing it can create. The body responds to the mind by manifesting whatever this destructive mind conjures up.

Meditation is a tool to help quiet this deranged part of your mind so you can relax and move into the present moment— the *now*. In the *now* moment, there is no lack or limitation, no bills to pay, no horror from yesterday, no terror in the future, and no horror sneaking up around the corner. There is only stillness, and in the still, now moment, you encounter God.

Stilling the mind is one of the hardest things to do on the spiritual path. Most beginners, like myself, have a tough time meditating. They cannot sit still and quiet the mind long enough to hear from God or any other spirit being wishing to communicate with you. This is why meditation must become part of your daily spiritual practice as well.

Most people who meditate receive spiritual messages that guide their entire day. Meditation is about accepting and recharging your energetic system. If you continue to struggle with meditation, pray, and ask God to give you direction for the best way to meditate. You do not have to sit in the lotus position with your eyes closed repeating, "*Ooooommmm.*" This is only one way to meditate. You can meditate with your eyes wide open. You can meditate staring at a candle. You can meditate lying down. You may recall my favorite way to meditate is floating on my back in the Caribbean Sea. I can do that for hours, and I always emerge from my meditations, feeling light and renewed. Do not let popular movies or anyone tell you how to meditate. Again, seek the method that is best for you. You can also try various methods until you find one that makes sense for you. Most importantly, be patient with yourself. DO NOT GIVE UP!

Journaling

Documentation, documentation, documentation! As a professor of social work and field instruction, I could not emphasize enough to my students the importance of documentation. These students were preparing for careers in public and private agencies dealing with people's lives. Documentation of everything transpiring between the worker and client was a must. I taught my students,

If it is not in black and white, it did not happen.

Therefore, I cannot emphasize more the importance of journaling as a daily spiritual practice. This is not a *dear diary* type of exercise. Keeping spiritual journals accomplish several essential functions. First, it helps you to keep track of your spiritual growth by recording your spiritual journey. If done consistently, journaling will provide you with a record of your spiritual progress. Second, your journal is an accountability tool. When you set an intention for yourself, write it in your journal. This will keep you honest by showing you whether or not you are being true to your word. Third, your journals are the place to record everything of value to you on your spiritual walk.

Who did you meet? Where did you meet them?
What miraculous thing happened today?
What new insights have you gained?
What are you grateful for?

Fourth, reflecting on your entries can give you new insights and guidance for the future. When you see how far you have come...keep going. Your journal will help motivate you more than any outside force because of the power of your intention. When you select your journal, make sure it is pretty or appealing to your eye. Treat yourself to an attractive journal. If you are creative, you can decorate your own. You can accentuate and/or personalize your journals any way you like. I tend to pick a journal that immediately jumps out at me or "*calls my name.*"

Your spiritual walk is worth documenting. No one is required to be interested in your life but you. Once you become comfortable with journaling, you will see how it is an outlet for your private spiritual expression. There are some things you may prefer to keep between you and God. Journaling is a non-judgment activity. If you find you are judging the entries in your journal, stop and begin self-forgiveness exercises. Journaling also helps you acknowledge your wins and losses. In this regard, it is a tool for correction. Correction is a must on every spiritual journey because we do not always know what we are doing or why we are doing it. Documenting your journey is a gentle form of self-correction. Purchase a pretty journal and put it to work for you today!

Body Movement

Your body was created to move. It must move to be fit. Most PBW recognize the importance of physical movement for the body. Some have gym memberships, others have walking groups, and some train for marathons. Most PBW pay attention to their health needs in this regard. Those who do not are more likely to experience energy blockages, stiffness, and weight gain. Physical health helps you to accomplish spiritual activities requiring strength and endurance. For example, on my spiritual retreat to Sedona, Arizona, we climbed up the side of Bell Rock, which is a mountain sitting directly on an energy vortex. What was supposed to be a one-hour field trip turned into a three-hour healing experience! I had to be physically able to climb up the mountain, overcome cold, wind, hunger, and fear sitting on the side of a mountain, all in the name of spiritual enlightenment. My life changed dramatically on Bell Rock, so I cannot complain.

Another dramatic healing experience occurred in a water temple in Bali, Indonesia. Before entering the water, I had to pray and ask permission from the temple spirits to enter the temple. Then, I had to climb down into the freezing water and stay there for what felt like an eternity to partake in the water ritual. Once I started, I was determined to finish. I had to have the physical ability to endure this process to receive my blessing. I would not have had this experience if my physical health prevented me from participating. Yes, daily physical activity is a constant spiritual practice. Some women reported practicing various forms of yoga. They suggested yoga is not merely exercise; it is also the practice of preparing the mind and body to enter a higher spiritual dimension. Some people practice stretching and other low-impact physical activities at home. This is also acceptable. Until you have reached enlightenment, keep your body active and moving.

Sacred Study

The Bible was the primary sacred text for the majority of PBW in the study. However, PBW on a spiritual path will naturally be drawn to other theological philosophies to answer or clarify deep spiritual questions. As you progress in your spiritual walk, you will cross paths with diverse religious and spiritual communities, all sharing their concept of God,

Supreme Being, Source, etc. Hopefully, these encounters will show you, regardless of the label, at the core of these belief systems is the belief in the concept of ONE Source of all things. It really does not matter what these cultures decide to call this ONE or Source. Of importance is the consensus of ONE Source from where everything flows.

Sacred study means you are open to learning and expanding your mind using sacred text, probably those forbidden by your church or pastor. Because spiritual people do not allow outside entities to limit their education, it is not surprising to find they have read other holy books such as the Quran, Torah, Bhagavad Gita, or Tripitakas. You might also be drawn to other sacred text like lost books of the Bible, The Protoevangelium, The Gospel of the Infancy of Jesus Christ, The Infancy Gospel of Thomas, The Epistles of Jesus Christ and Abgarus King of Edessa, The Gospel of Nicodemus, Acts of Pilate, The Apostles' Creed, The Epistle of Paul the Apostle to the Laodiceans, and many, many more. One of the truths you will discover on your spiritual journey is how much you don't know. There is always so much more to learn or revisit. Therefore, it is vital to dedicate a portion of your day to sacred study. Remain open and teachable. Before you reject something, ask yourself,

What part of my consciousness is rejecting this information?

Energy Work

Energy work entails moving energy around and through the body's energetic zones (e.g., meridians and chakras). Some achieve this through the use of breath and by balancing the chakras. Others use Qi Gong and Tai Chi and other eastern spiritual traditions to move energy through major energy portals on the body. These practices are gaining wider popularity, especially among PBW. More Black women are traveling abroad to study and become masters in traditional eastern treatment and healing modalities.

EFT (Emotional Freedom Techniques)

EFT is an ancient holistic eastern (Chinese) healing and stress relief practice. One of my coaches and master teacher of EFT describes it as *"acupuncture without the pins."* This technique uses *"tapping"* throughout the *"energetic meridians"* on the body to reduce low vibrational expressions such as stress, anger, fear, anxiety, depression, etc. By tapping lightly on seven (7) specific energy centers on the body (ex.: over the eye, side of the eye, under the eye, under the nose, over the chin, over the collarbone, under the arm, over the heart, and top of the head), you can move energy through these portals on the body. When you can clear this blocked or stagnant energy in your body, you may be able to overcome pain and discomfort, and other dis-eases in the body.

You can sense when energy is blocked in your body. It is typically expressed by feeling tired and exhausted all the time. EFT uses scripts or short sayings that are recited as you tap on the energy centers. The purpose of the scripts is to force your subconscious mind to align with what you truly want to manifest. The tapping signals the mind to move energy through the body's *"energetic meridians."* Listen to your body and respond appropriately before the blocked energy escalates into a significant health problem or dis-ease.

Events and Retreats

Problems are not geographical. You take them wherever you go. Healing, on the other hand, is geographical. You cannot experience spiritual healing from your couch or your armchair. You cannot experience true healing from reading self-help books or binge-watching YouTube videos. You must have a visceral experience, meaning all five of your senses must be engaged to alert your subconscious mind the body is having an extraordinary experience. Attending spiritual events and retreats will take you to many places and spaces on earth specifically designed for your healing. If you can envision yourself retreating in an international destination, there is a part of your consciousness that is already there. It is your job to say yes to your healing experience and catch up with the part of your consciousness that is already there.

What are you healing from? You are healing from the negative narrative of lack and limitation. You are healing from a consciousness that has tricked you into believing you cannot travel from here to there for whatever reason. Your soul knows exactly what it needs to flourish. If your soul requires being on a beach for healing, it will somehow find a way to get your body there.

Five Sense

Aromatherapy (Smell) uses essential oils, incense, and other natural fragrances to enhance the atmosphere and appeal to the olfactory. Aromas can change your experience from negative to positive. Also, various scents invite or entertain benevolent spirits and entities. If you are doing angel work, specific fragrances are more appealing to particular angels.

These fragrances are like an invitation welcoming these energies. Some scents are used for protecting, raising your vibration, and attracting love, money, and good fortune. You know the difference between smelling something beautiful and smelling something yucky, so do the entities in the unseen world. I only use high-quality essential oils in my spiritual practice.

Massage (Touch) is an essential part of healing. It connects your energy with another. It is natural for you to desire good touch. Some people do not like to be touched. This should be examined carefully with a coach or trusted spiritual leader who would be willing to explore where the issue of negative touch began. Jesus laid hands on the sick, and they recovered. If touch was effective for Jesus, it should be effective for you too. Some people have entire healing ministries based on touch or healing hands. I love whole body massages as well as target areas such as my feet and back.

Sight (Vision) what do you see all around you? Is your immediate environment what you want to see, or is it something else? The atmosphere around you is simply a projection of your subconscious mind. If you do not like the *out-picturing* of what you see, you have to change your subconscious mind. It takes time to change the subconscious mind. Some PBW trick their subconscious mind by putting up pictures in their office of locations they would rather be.

As a stress relief, they stare at a view of the beach, mountains, rainforest, etc. like a mini escape from reality. This is an effective hack but not more effective than experiencing the real thing. I have been calling myself *"Dr. B on the Beach"* for years before I ever lived on the beach, and somehow the beach is where I now call home. I get to stare at crystal blue waters as my daily spiritual practice.

Sound (Healing Tones) is very important to the soul. The universe and everything in it was created by sound. God spoke, and it was. You cannot afford to discount the importance of sound. Sound can change your atmosphere in a split second. Practice waking up to your favorite inspirational music. Think about how you feel when you are having a bad day (e.g., low vibrational), and you hear your favorite song. In an instant, your mood goes from low vibrational to high vibrational. Now you are singing and snapping your fingers (movement) rhythmically, and in no time, you are feeling much better. Sound can clear your atmosphere of negative energies and heal your body (e.g., solfeggio tones). If you ever want to raise your vibe, put on your favorite, positive, high vibrational songs, and enjoy.

Taste (high vibrational food) is connected to one of the basic needs-food. All food has a vibration-high or low. High vibrational foods are those closest to nature and unadulterated by man. Low vibrational foods are man-made processed food. There is a difference between food grown naturally and in season and food grown on large industrial farms available in all seasons. Most of these foods are genetically altered, such that they do not contain a marked level of nutrition. A diet low of vibrational food can cause sickness and disease to enter the body. The things that are good for us usually do not taste good. You have to be intentional about the foods you consume, especially on a spiritual journey.

In preparation for my Ayahuasca rituals in Peru, we were instructed to eat a vegan or close to a vegan diet to cleanse our digestive systems. We were forbidden to eat any type of meat, especially pork. This was not an issue for me as it was for other retreaters. I do not eat pork at all. However, the ban on sugar and sweets was a real struggle for me.

Personal Care

Personal care can be just about anything you decide to do to enhance your life experience. Silence is one example. Many spiritual leaders spend an enormous amount of time in silence. When I am in silence, I have to find a means of non-verbal communication to assist me. Silence is a great way to listen to your thoughts and hear what pops up. Instead of chatting with friends or gossiping, you can use silence to bring you to a place of calm. You can journal your experiences in silence.

Self-love

Self-love is a must as a part of your daily spiritual practice. Self-love is a deep appreciation for your life and the chance to appreciate your uniqueness. Self-appreciation stems from your ability to love *Self*. When you encounter a person with a negative disposition, you may think that person does not love him or herself. Or if they are angry or mean, you may think only hurting people can hurt others. Yes! Lack of self-love is detected in your self-talk. Love yourself more. Self-love is a must because you will encounter aspects of yourself that you simply do not like. It is in these moments where self-forgiveness, a component of self-love, helps. Whatever you are holding, anger, guilt, or shame about this practice will identify areas of your life in need of forgiveness. The spiritual antidote for self-loathing is self-love.

Spiritual Communities

Spiritual communities are essential to your spiritual journey. Though some may think being spiritual requires intense, prolonged periods of solitude, it also involves the community. Your spiritual quest may be lonely at times. You may feel the need to withdraw and be quiet. However, there is an aspect of healing that can only occur when in a relationship with others. Individuals you encounter on your journey are mirrors reflecting hidden aspects of yourself that require healing or celebrating. If you are single and think you have reached a high state of spiritual development, get into an intimate relationship. This person will give you invaluable information about the hidden aspects of yourself. They are called your "*highly paid consultants.*" Learning from this type of relationship can propel you to a higher level of spiritual growth and save you money and hours on a therapist's couch.

Spiritual communities exist online and in person. The development of new communication technology allows people to connect worldwide. Many people feel safer to express their spirituality in closed groups online. This is also a place to go if you are seeking to connect with like-minded people. Online offers flexibility for meeting globally and the opportunity for viewing recorded sessions at your convenience. It is essential to find spiritual friends who love you most of all, they "*get you.*"

Vibration Attunement

God created the earth with numerous high vibrational places for healing and rejuvenation. It is your responsibility to get out of your regular routine and decide to travel to those locations to receive the healing waiting for you. Sedona,

Arizona is a prime example of an energy vortex in the United States where people travel worldwide to have healing experiences. You have to feel it for yourself to become real in your body, mind, and soul.

Visioning

It is time to throw out your vision boards and hop on over to the spiritual practice of visioning. Vision boards are limited to the things already in your consciousness. However, visioning is sitting in meditation and allowing God to channel through you, things you could never conceive with your human mind. Visioning pushes you beyond what you already know to be open and receptive to the miraculous. The Bible expresses this sentiment in the following verse:

> *But as it is written, eye hath not seen, nor ear heard, neither has entered into the heart of man, the things which God hath prepared for them that love Him.*
> *(1 Corinthians 2:9)*

God demonstrates the things that are prepared for you have not even been placed in your consciousness. The practice of visioning allows you to tap into this unseen world to glimpse God's vision for your life. Vision boards cannot accomplish this; visioning can.

Spiritual self-care includes all practices aimed at raising your vibration, bringing you closer to God, the Universe, your Higher Self, or whatever you connect to spiritually. Spiritual self-care includes, but is not limited to, a commitment to a daily spiritual practice, care for the physical body, mastering energy, participation in a spiritual community, and events and retreats. Path-seekers at every level know spiritual self-care practices help you to return to a more natural way of being. You can expect greater vitality and zest for life, even when things look really, really bleak. Those experienced in spiritual self-care know nothing stays the same—everything changes. Having a secure connection to your spiritual base ends stress. It is time you encounter the knowing that you live in an abundant benevolent universe that is here to serve you. You have angels for protection. You have spiritual gifts to share. Knowing you are deeply loved will, in time, end all stress in your life.

Spells are just prayers with more steps and a name that scares people. — Lily Anderson

19 CHAPTER 19

THE SPELLS

DISCLAIMER   DISCLAIMER   DISCLAIMER

You are sovereign. Your energy and vibe are your own. You bring your energy to every situation. Therefore, you MUST pray and ask Spirit for guidance with ALL spiritual practices or rituals. What works for me may not work for you and vice versa. Everything I am sharing with you can be researched further online, in books, or with your spiritual community. I am not personally or professionally endorsing the use of ANY of the spells provided in the chapter. The information is descriptive, not prescriptive. If you do want to try any of these spells, please pray and do your research first. You can contact me (via email) for a deeper dive into your questions.

Professional Black women reported using spirituality as a resource for coping most frequently for help with protection, direction, money, and romance. The spells in this chapter provide examples of Psalms, Candle Magick, and Sacred Baths in ritual work.

Psalms

Psalms are a collection of poems and songs sung to God for praise, thanksgiving, supplication, adoration, exhortation, lamentation, and wisdom. Most were written by King David of Israel. They are found in the Torah or the Old Testament of the Bible. Among the occult, Psalms are used to appeal to God for divine intervention in human affairs. For every situation, there is a Psalm to address the need. Psalms are included here because most PBW were raised in the Judeo-Christian faith and are very familiar with the power of the Psalms.

Candle Magick

Most religions incorporate candles in worship and spiritual practice. As indicated before, I was introduced to candles in the Catholic Church. We lit candles to pray for our dearly departed and our patron saints. We also lit candles to pray for those in purgatory. The Catholics believe in purgatory, and they believe you can light candles to pray for people up to heaven with the energy of the candles. Candle use is a staple in most religious and spiritual practices. When they are used in traditional churches and other mainstream celebrations, they are acceptable. When used in occult practices, they are considered harmful and spooky. On the spiritual side, candles are considered a powerful spiritual implement because they represent the altars' fire element. Candles use the energy of fire as the transformational power to burning off negativity and bringing forth positive, energetic change to your life.

Sacred Baths

Sacred baths bring the energy of the water element to your spiritual practice. Spiritual baths can include plants, flowers, essential oils, candles, and sacred reading. Almost any bathing routine allowing you to raise your vibration and feel good about yourself, can be considered a sacred bath (Sherman, 2016). Sacred baths will enable you to wash off negative energy so you can bask in the positive energy you do want to experience. Sacred baths are medicine to the soul. If you are experiencing a low vibration, prepare a nice bath, light some candles, and enjoy. All the spells provided are spells you can do on your own.

Magick Spells

Protection

Until you rise to a Level 3 or 4 in consciousness, it is likely you still believe there is something outside of you that is out to get you on the job. You are still in victim mode, believing you need to be protected from something. If this is where you are, it is quite ok. Until you are operating at a higher level of consciousness, it might be best to learn some protection spells for the workplace.

Spell #1: Psalms for Protection

Use Psalm 12

When a vicious or jealous person spreads falsehood, which may harm, write the names of the rumormonger on the four edges of a square of parchment.

1. **Copy verse 3 in the center of the paper.**

2. Fold a paper in half away from you and then in half again in the other direction.

3. Pin it together so it will not become unfolded.

4. Bury it, as close to the vicious one's property as soon as possible and the lies will soon cease.

Psalms 12

1 Help, Lord, for no one is faithful anymore;
those who are loyal have vanished from the human race.
2 Everyone lies to their neighbor;
they flatter with their lips
but harbor deception in their hearts.
3 May the Lord silence all flattering lips
and every boastful tongue—
4 those who say,
"By our tongues we will prevail;
our own lips will defend us—who is lord over us?"
5 "Because the poor are plundered and the needy groan,
I will now arise," says the Lord.
"I will protect them from those who malign them."
6 And the words of the Lord are flawless,
like silver purified in a crucible,
like gold[c] refined seven times.
7 You, Lord, will keep the needy safe
and will protect us forever from the wicked,
8 who freely strut about
when what is vile is honored by the human race.

Source: Power of Psalms (p. 15)

Spell #2: Candle Magick

Commanding Respect at a Meeting With Supervisors

1. Use Psalms 5.

1. Assemble any paperwork, documentation, writing tablets, or things you will carry into your meeting with the executive, manager, or boss.

2. Fix a purple or yellow candle with commanding oil.

3. Write the executive, manager, or boss's in the candle with a needle and speak your intention.

5. Prepare a paper with the name (and photo, if you can get it) of the person you desire to respect and write their names and your proposal you wish to be granted.

6. Put the paper under the candle.

7. Light the candle and, working only by its light, assemble items and the clothes and jewelry you will be wearing to the meeting.

8. Light incense.

9. Prepare a bath and dissolve commanding sachet powders, oil, or bath crystals in water.

10. As you dissolve the bath oil or bath crystals, recite Psalm 5 to find favor with authorities or superiors in business.

11. When complete, snuff (do not blow) out the candles and go to sleep.

In the morning...

1. Relight the candle and recite **Psalms 5** again.

2. Put on the prepared clothes and jewelry.

3. Take the name paper out from under the candle and write Psalms 5 all over it in your own handwriting.

4. Place the paper in the shoe of your dominant foot.

5. Add a pinch of salt for *protection*, sugar to s*weeten the person*, cinnamon powder for *money*, John the Conqueror root for *willpower*, and gravel root, for *favor on the job*.

6. If you have a safe place to keep the candle burning while you are at the meeting, do so. A bathtub, fireplace, or kitchen sink is generally safe. The candle will back you up while you are at the meeting.

7. Walk into the meeting carrying your dressed and prepared materials stepping on the name of the executive, commanding him to do as you.
wish.

Psalms 5

1 Listen to my words, Lord,
consider my lament.
2 Hear my cry for help,
my King and my God,
for to you I pray.
3 In the morning, Lord, you hear my voice;
in the morning I lay my requests before you
and wait expectantly.
4 For you are not a God who is pleased with wickedness;
with you, evil people are not welcome.
5 The arrogant cannot stand
in your presence.
You hate all who do wrong;
6 you destroy those who tell lies.
The bloodthirsty and deceitful
you, Lord, detest.
7 But I, by your great love,
can come into your house;
in reverence I bow down
toward your holy temple.
8 Lead me, Lord, in your righteousness
because of my enemies—
make your way straight before me.
9 Not a word from their mouth can be trusted;
their heart is filled with malice.
Their throat is an open grave;
with their tongues they tell lies.
10 Declare them guilty, O God!
Let their intrigues be their downfall.
Banish them for their many sins,
for they have rebelled against you.
11 But let all who take refuge in you be glad;
let them ever sing for joy.

Spread your protection over them,
that those who love your name may rejoice in you.
12 Surely, Lord, you bless the righteous;
you surround them with your favor as with a shield.

Spell #3: Sacred Bath of Least Resistance

Self-care is the best protection from stress on the job. This beautiful Bath of Least Resistance allows you to surrender to Spirit and trust yourself more on the job. Relax, breathe, and luxuriate in this bath, knowing all your stress will be washed down the drain.

Bath Recipe
- 4 drops of lavender oil
- 4 drops of Roman chamomile oil
- 4 drops of frankincense oil
- Clear quartz crystal or Rhodochrosite
- One cup of apple cider vinegar or Epsom salt
- Holy basil tea

Explanation of Bath Elements
- Lavender oil balances the emotions
- Roman chamomile oil is relaxing and good to release resistance and tension.
- Frankincense oil for spiritual grounding
- Clear quartz crystal or Rhodochrosite for mental clarity
- Apple cider vinegar or Epsom salt for cleansing.
- Holy basil tea to uplift your spirit.

Procedure:

1. Clean and clear your atmosphere with prayer and incense.

2. Give ALL your work-related challenges temporarily over to the Divine.

3. Practice having faith in a Higher Power.

4. Learn to work with the Universe instead of fighting things. Admit when you do not know, so a better way can emerge.

5. Surrender all possible attachments to need to be right. This will raise your vibration beyond your ego and allow you to walk them in peace.

6. Breathe and Relax

Direction

PBW invariably desire insight about the direction of their careers and their overall life path. They want to know if they will get a promotion or if a promotion is what they want. Should they resign from a horrible job situation, or should they stick it out until something else shows up? In today's job climate, more PBW are choosing to seek spiritual guidance for direction in their careers. Many have found it has made a difference (Sherman, 2016).

Direction Spell #1: Psalms 32: 8-11

Procedures:

1. Use Psalms 32 early in the morning.
   Use a compass to find EAST.
2. Facing EAST and recite verse 8-11 one time.
3. Facing SOUTH and repeat verse 8-11 one time.
4. Facing WEST and repeat verse 8-11 one time.
5. Facing NORTH and repeat verse 8-11 one time.
6. On a clean sheet of white paper write Psalms 32: 8:11 in your handwriting using a purple pen.
7. Place it under a WHITE candle facing EAST for 7 days
8. After 7 days, remove the paper and burn it in your cauldron or release it in running water like a river.
9. Expect information is coming to you concerning the direction you must go.

Psalms 32: 8:11

8 The Lord says, "I will teach you the way you should go;
I will instruct you and advise you.
9 Don't be stupid like a horse or a mule,
which must be controlled with a bit and bridle
to make it submit."
10 The wicked will have to suffer,
but those who trust in the Lord
are protected by his constant love.
11 You that are righteous, be glad and rejoice
because of what the Lord has done.
You that obey him, shout for joy!

Direction Spell #2: Candle

Procedure:

1. Use a YELLOW candle. Yellow candles help you manifest your desires, bring mental clarity, and bring your desires to fruition.

2. Clean the candle with Florida Water and anoint it with olive oil.

3. Set up your altar with all four elements: cup (water), air (incense), fire (your candle), earth (stones, rocks, crystals). You may include an iron element for protection.

4. Place items on a white altar cloth. Use an encased candle.

5. Write out your intention for this ritual. For example, *"I intend to obtain direction for my next step on the job."*

6. Light candle and incense.

7. Sit and pray or play your favorite spiritual music.

8. When you feel a release. Arise.

9. Allow the candle to burn down. Remove from the altar when done. This may take time, depending on the size of the candle.

9. Take the paper you wrote your intention on and burn it. Place the ashes in your cauldron.

10. Thank God for your answer and wait for it to manifest.

11. DO NOT BLOW out the candle. Snuff the candle out.

Bath Recipe

- 4 drops of frankincense oil
- 4 drops of patchouli oil
- 3 drops of myrrh oil
- 1 drop of clove oil
- Clear quartz or aventurine
- Green candle
- One cup of apple cider vinegar or one cup of Epsom salt
- Kava, juniper berry, or Patchouli tea

Explanation of the Bath Elements

- Frankincense oil is spiritual grounding.
- Patchouli oil is great for money, fertility, and uplifting the mind.
- Myrrh oil uplifts emotions and provides spiritual awareness.
- Clove oil is good for abundance.
- Clear Quartz/Aventurine attracts new opportunities and helps to overcome self-doubt.
- Green candle for wealth abundance
- Apple cider vinegar or one cup Epsom salt for cleansing
- Kava, juniper berry, or Patchouli tea to uplift your spirit.

Ritual

1. Perform this ritual in the AM only.

2. Light a green candle and invite in Lakshmi, the goddess of abundance and your guardian angel.

3. Pray to Lakshmi as you look at the flame of your green candle, which is the color for money and the unlimited love in your heart.

4. See yourself as a magnet for All your desires.

5. Take 15 minutes to decide what you wish to create. See it in detail as if it's happening now.

6. Welcome prosperity into your life.

7. Allow any doubt, fear, or obstacles to drain out of the tub with the bathwater, so they are no longer in your energy field.

8. Ask Lakshmi to surround you with the green light of success in the matter.

9. Affirm: *"I am worthy of all my dreams, and I'm now ready to manifest them."*
10. Snuff out the green candle. DO NOT BLOW OUT THE CANDLE.

11. Relax and drink your tea for peace and pleasure.

12. Journal about the guidance you received from your session. (Sherman, 2016).

Romance

PBW desire love and romance in their lives. They feel they have invested so much into themselves, and they are ready for a suitable mate. Those who are impatient have gone so far as to assume the male role in the relationship or simply do too much. Doing too much leads to disagreements, disappointment, and sometimes a court case. Some women hold out for their dream mate and others may decide to use spiritual means to expedite the process.

All of these spells are predicated upon your belief and clear intention. If you are an unkind person, you will only draw an unkind person to you. Even if the person is nice, you will probably experience the unkind part of this person's characteristics. When it comes to romance, it is best to ONLY spell yourself. Raise your vibration so you will only attract to you someone of your emotional complement. Be very careful with these types of spells. Make sure you are not attempting to override someone else's will. Good luck!

Spell for Romance #1: Psalms

Procedures:
1. Clean and clear a PINK candle.

2. Anoint the candle with olive oil.

3. Carve the name of the object of your desire on the candle. If you are using an encased candle, write the name in PINK ink on a clean white piece of paper and place it under the candle.

4. Arise before 6:00 am. Light the candle and recite Psalm 48 three times.

5. Write out Psalm 48 write once on a clean sheet of white paper. Use PINK ink if possible.

6. Repeat for seven days.

7. DO NOT BLOW out the candle. Snuff the candle out.

Psalm 48

1 Great is the Lord, and most worthy of praise,
in the city of our God, his holy mountain.
2 Beautiful in its loftiness,
the joy of the whole earth,
like the heights of Zaphon is Mount Zion,
the city of the Great King.
3 God is in her citadels;
he has shown himself to be her fortress.
4 When the kings joined forces,
when they advanced together,
5 they saw her and were astounded;
they fled in terror.
6 Trembling seized them there,
pain like that of a woman in labor.
7 You destroyed them like ships of Tarshish
shattered by an east wind.
8 As we have heard,
so, we have seen
in the city of the Lord Almighty,
in the city of our God:
God makes her secure
forever.
9 Within your temple, O God,

we meditate on your unfailing love.
10 Like your name, O God,
your praise reaches to the ends of the earth;
your right hand is filled with righteousness.
11 Mount Zion rejoices,
the villages of Judah are glad
because of your judgments.
12 Walk about Zion, go around her,
count her towers,
13 consider well her ramparts,
view her citadels,
that you may tell of them
to the next generation.
14 For this God is our God forever and ever;
He will be our guide even to the end.

Spell for Romance#2: Clean Slate Sacred Bath

Demographically, a disproportionate number PBW are single, head of household. Of those who are divorced, the remarriage rate is dismally low. PBW face numerous barriers dating or starting over in romance. Learn the lessons from your past relationships, so you do not repeat them going forward. Make sure you are ready for romance and not rebound. Give yourself time, and when you are ready, prepare this sacred bath. This sacred bath is geared to give you a clean slate from the past and put you in the mind frame to be open to a new love by loving yourself (Sherman, 2016).

Bath Recipe

- 2 drops of hyssop oil
- 4 drops of lavender oil
- 3 drops of rose oil
- Rhodochrosite
- White candle
- 1 cup of sea salt for cleansing
- Rosehip tea

Explanation of Bath Elements

- Hyssop oil releases negativity so you can forgive.
- Lavender oil balances your energy.
- Rose oil stimulates love, peace, and an open heart. Rhodochrosite crystal cleanses the heart.
- White candle is for peace and forgiveness.
- Sea salt for cleansing.
- Rosehip tea

Bath Ritual

1. Begin in the morning (if possible).

2. Light a white candle and ask archangel Zadkiel to assist you in forgiving all past love partners. Archangel Zadkiel can help you to develop compassion towards yourself and others. He is the Archangel of transformation, freedom, and mercy.

3. Allow the Divine energy of compassionate release to fill your tub.

4. Breathe it in. Lie in the aromatic water and bring up the faces of your past partners who have disappointed or hurt you.

5. Take the love-filled bathwater and splash it on their imaginary faces saying,

May your memory be cleansed.
May your being be purified and freed and may both of our
hearts be released of any hurt so only peace remains.
So may it be.

6. Ask Archangel Zadkiel to cut any etheric energy cords of fear between you and the other person or persons.

7. Allow yourself to know lightness and peace in your heart. Take a moment to bless each soul and allow every person to move on to their highest good, acknowledging that their being wishes you the same in return.

8. Thank Archangel Zadkiel for assisting so you can love with more lightness and purity of heart.

9. Allow the leftover resentment, pain, or negative memories to go down the drain for good. Thank yourself for having the courage to do this.

10. Snuff out the white candle. DO NOT BLOW OUT THE CANDLE.

11. After the bath, sip some rosehip tea and breathe deeply and relax. Document your insights in your Love Journal.

Spell #3: Solfeggio Love Meditation

1. Prepare your space to usher in Love and Compassion. You may use PINK and WHITE candles.
2. Light jasmine or lavender incense.
3. Access YouTube online.
4. Charge up your love crystals on your altar and hold them in your hands during the Love Meditation (e.g.: clear quartz, rose quartz, rhodonite, garnet)

5. Use the links provided to find these YouTube videos below.
6. Enjoy...

Pure Positive Love Energy Miracle Tone Healing Music | Heart Chakra

Solfeggio Frequency

https://youtu.be/5T_QxR8aclQ
Harmonize Relationships, Heal Old Negative Energy, Attract Love, Solfeggio Healing Tones
https://youtu.be/H1zGk4GcuqQ
Attract Love, Raise Positive Energy, Meditation Music
https://youtu.be/yiGweP--BRs

Money Manifestation

Money, money, money...Money! You are living in a material world. Money is what you exchange for the things you believe you need and want. Do you have a scary relationship with money? Do you chase away money by saying something like,

I'm broke.
Money doesn't grow on trees.
Where do you think I am supposed to get the money from?

What you need to understand is money is energy. It is a spirit and operates by spiritual law. It has its own vibration, and the vibration is high. Paper money is magical and mystical. It was created as a symbol of trust and is used as a symbol of this energy.

Enlightened people with money are usually very high vibrational people. They are happy about attracting money and know to never chase away money with any word or deed. Low vibrating people continuously say negative things about money. Whatever they say will be. If you say,

I don't have money."
The universe says,
So mote it be.
If you say,
I'm saving money just in case something happens.

Guess what? Something is guaranteed to happen that will cost you probably precisely the same sum you saved. This occurs by universal law. Scan your mind now and think about how you talk about money.

One of the first things I had to learn on my spiritual journey was how to manifest money. I was not about to go crawling back into the *matrix*, so something had to happen. There are several ways to manifest money. I have tried a few, and they absolutely work. The most important thing to know is you already have everything. All the money you will ever need on earth is already present. Money is a tool to purchase your daily bread. You are still alive today whether or not you had money yesterday or last year. Money worries will drive money further and further away from you, by law.

Money is Your Servant.

Money is here to serve you. You should not be working for money. Money should be working for you. How? Start studying money. Purchase a beautiful journal you will designate as your *"wealth grimoire."* It does not have to be expensive; it gives you a feeling of richness when you see it and touch it. You can bling out a plain journal if you are crafty. The most important task is to clean and clear your wealth grimoire. You can place it on your wealth altar to charge up until you are ready to use it.

Below are the steps you can use to increase the flow of currency or money in my life. All I can say is, this stuff works!

Spell #1: Bible Scripture

1. Cleanse yourself and still your mind.
2. Breathe...
3. Prepare your atmosphere with prayer, solfeggio tones, and/or incense.
4. Read the scripture aloud 3 times and 3 times to yourself in the first person. Breathe.

5. Use: **2 Corinthians 9:8**

> *And* **God is able** *to bless you* **abundantly**, *so that in* **all things** *at* **all times**, **having all** *that you need, you* **will abound** *in every good work.*

5. **Spend time** really **meditating** on this scripture.
6. Look at each word and allow them to resound within you.

6. **Write down everything** that is revealed to you in your *wealth journal.*

Spell #2: Money Mantra

Mantras are specific, powerful, repetitive words and sounds used to penetrate the substrate of your subconscious mind and throughout the entire body. They are positive affirmations statements used to *craft* your physical world through sound vibration. Mantras are activated when chanted out loud, in meditation, listening to them, or my favorite, writing them down repeatedly. Mantras motivate you to become your best self by affirming something positive about yourself or your circumstances. They are a way to bring positive things into your life and give you focus on achieving your goal.

I learned about money mantras from a book of 40 money mantras (Love, 2017). I will share two of my favorite mantras with you. I use the first mantra to forgive myself for all my money mistakes. I must forgive myself because I have done some very unexpected things with my money. Let's just say these things were not wise or spirit led. I am sure I am not the only one who can admit to mismanaging personal funds. Actively forgiving myself for my money mishaps is essential to my present money flow. These old negative money beliefs are programs that must be deleted if I can trust myself with large sums of money again.

The second money mantra reminds me I can manifest anything. It reminds me I require nothing. If I want something, I manifest it like Jesus did. Jesus did not plan or schedule His miracles. He filled needs as He encountered them. Jesus did not store up for rainy days. He manifested whatever He wanted, whenever and wherever He wanted. I want to manifest, just like Jesus.

Steps

1. Clear and cleanse your mind of any negativity, especially towards money or your current finances.
2. Enhance the mood and atmosphere with candles (green for money) and incense (optional).
3. Relax and breathe.
4. Set your intention in your heart.
5. Recite or write out the mantra.
6. Allow Spirit to guide you as to what to do next.
7. Write everything down in your wealth grimoire.

Mantra #1: Day 26 Forgiven

I choose to deeply and radically forgive myself for EVERYTHING. Every error, mistake, misstep, and error miscalculation I have ever made with money is hereby FORGIVEN.
I forgive me and all I've done that did not align with my money manifestation and wealth creation.
I am free. It feels good to let me off the hook!
I AM FORGIVEN.
FOR EVERYTHING.
ASE

Mantra #2: Day 34 Multiply

I AM grateful to manifest like Christ. The moment there is
a requirement to be filled, I simply look to Heaven, offer
thanks, and break my bread
I use what is already present in my world and multiply it
into MORE THAN ENOUGH, simply by my THANKS
and FAITH. I know I always have more than I require for
all I desire. I know the UNI-VERSE MULTIPLIES my
GOOD exponentially. I know there is multiplying POWER
in my consciousness of thanks and praise.
Multiply me!
And so it is!

Spell #3: Solfeggio Tones for Abundance

Solfeggio tones are used to subliminally create a mindset of abundance and wealth. There are a plethora of YouTube videos with meditations recorded at 528Hz. Feel free to discover the abundance of videos on YouTube.

Steps

1. Clean and cleanse yourself.
2. Light a green or white candle (or both).
3. Burn your favorite money drawing incense.
4. Hold your money crystal or stone in your hands during the meditation and carry it in your wallet/purse when fully charged up (optional).
5. Play your favorite 528Hz Solfeggio audio or video, preferably using headphones.
6. Relax....
7. Record any insights in your wealth grimoire.

YouTube Videos

Millionaire Mindset Subliminal Affirmations for Wealth & Abundance - Alpha (10hz) Binaural Beats
https://youtu.be/evXhjHbTyNc

Attract Abundance of Money Prosperity Luck & Wealth; Jupiter's Spin Frequency; Theta Binaural Beats https://youtu.be/PEJRmo6QubY

"Money Flows To You" Attract Wealth Meditation, Miracle Happens While You Sleep, Money Magnet
https://youtu.be/azoM-E7D7PI

I would encourage you to do your research and find magick spells that fit your needs. I mentioned all of these spells were curated for you as a beginning place for your spiritual work. It is up to you to determine what you need for yourself. And if you do not know, spend some more time in prayer and meditation and ask God. God created you, and God knows how to love, provide, and care for you best. You Are Not Alone. There are so many others who would love to connect with you on your spiritual journey. You can connect with other spiritual sisters and brothers who will help you along the way. I wish you the best and pray you continue to work on your *self* so you will only attract the things you truly want in your life. Indeed, self-care and self-love are the ultimate magick spells.

Take this job and shove it…I ain't working here no more!
David Allan Coe

20 CHAPTER 20

MAYA'S TRANSITION

Maya was the first person in her family to graduate with a master's degree in business administration. Her educational preparation and leadership skills landed her a dream job working for a large corporation. Maya's investment in her education had paid off. Even though she had an enormous student loan to repay, she had everything she had hoped for—a cushy, high paying corporate career, the respect of her family and friends, support from her peers, and a suitable husband. Life was great.

Ten years into her employment, Maya finally had to admit she was miserable. She realized her core values were not aligned with those of the corporation. Maya valued harmony and inclusiveness in the workspace knowing profit was the bottom line and the company's only concern. She especially did not like the way lower-ranking employees were treated. She witnessed years of racial and gender discrimination, employee mistreatment, and unfair promotion practices towards certain employees. Although she did not directly experience the mistreatment, she could not help but think she was being spared the harassment because of her fair complexion and growing up in an upper-middle-class Black family. Some of her White co-workers made comments in passing that she was *different* than the other African American women in the company.

As a deeply empathetic person, riddled with guilt because her white colleagues gave her preferential treatment, Maya wondered how much longer she could survive in this work environment. She often felt defeated because even though she did not like what was going on, she needed her hefty paycheck. After a defining incident when she stood up for a subordinate, upper management chastised her for *overstepping* her bounds and reminded her of her *"specialness."* She was fed up and knew something had to change radically or else. Every day she wanted to quit, but she had accumulated so much debt from purchasing a luxury car, a more massive than necessary home, student loans, and constantly supporting her less fortunate family members. Maya was so bogged down in debt; she could not see any other option than to keep working this high-stress job. Maya knew she had long lost the enthusiasm for the job when she accepted the position ten years ago.

In year twelve, Maya was diagnosed with high blood pressure. Long hours at the office, overextending herself with public service activities, and her increasingly miserable disposition began to wear on her marriage. She was going through so much at work and needed an outlet to release stress. Her husband did not fully understand what she was experiencing. He tried to be supportive, but he saw things differently. Maya did not feel supported, so she stopped sharing her feelings with him. The marriage began to suffer. Maya felt her entire life was falling apart and she did not know what to do. She could not tell her family about the troubles on the job or her marital issues. All of her family and close friends loved her husband. He was a great guy. She could not let them down. She tried to fix the marriage, but nothing was working.

One day Maya came back from lunch to find a human resources administrator waiting outside of her large office. The HR administrator handed her an envelope containing a termination letter. Maya was fired. The letter simply stated the company is going in a different direction, and her services were no longer required. Maya went blank. She did not know whether to be relieved or terrified. She panicked. Depression set in. She was so exhausted that she spent most of her days sleeping, crying, or eating. Her husband tried to be supportive. He felt she should get back on the job market right away. He felt this would be the best way for her to get out of her rut. Maya disagreed. She did not want to sign up for more of the same nonsense that drove her to her present condition. She stayed in bed and watched YouTube videos hoping she would find something inspirational to motivate her.

The Mind Shift

Many PBW get to this point in their careers, where they experience all the signs to exit the job matrix. Yet, they are waiting for something monumental to happen as the *sign* to move on. For Maya, it was getting fired, a failing marriage, and accumulating health problems. Maya's awakening to her spiritual journey began when she stopped feeling sorry for herself and began online transformational coaching. After getting to know, like, and trust this coach online, Maya decided to attend an in-person weekend retreat. The retreat was designed for women (like Maya) who had exited corporate America and needed support taking the next steps. The retreat was motivational and inspirational, precisely what she needed to begin her journey. Maya also felt the need to connect to her real life's purpose instead of competing in corporate America. She wanted to be a *"way-shower"* for other talented women in corporate America who were contemplating exiting the *"rat race."*

Maya focused on acquiring detailed information on exactly *how* to transfer the skills she used successfully working a job to this new lifestyle of a *motivational entrepreneur*. Though she was focused and organized, she needed personal and spiritual development to change her mind from feeling like a *victim* to *being* the creative director of her life. Maya worked for five years with her coach while she made her transition to her new life. Today, Maya is healthy and happily married to the same man. Her work inspires many women to follow their hearts and consider pursuing the dream life they deserve outside of corporate America. She is living her dream by sharing her experiences. This was what she envisioned her life would look like, and she was finally there. She had the dream life she deserve outside of corporate America.

21 CHAPTER 21

FROM WORKING TO LIVING

At some point you realize the plan you created for your life is not working. You realize you are torturing yourself in a job that is draining you, and it is getting worse. You are tired of working to pay off a huge mortgage, high car note(s), and education costs. Money is flying out of your bank accounts like crazy, and you just do not know what to do. Maybe you might be willing to consider another route out of the hell you created for yourself.

> *What are you going to do now?*
> *Is Jesus coming to pay all of your bills?*
> *Are you scheduled to win the lottery?*
> *What are your options?*

There are only two options—your plan and God's plan. **Figure 6** shows the dichotomy between God's plan and your plan. God's plan is fueled by trust, love, patience, and faith. It requires you to surrender your will, meaning all of your bright ideas, and allow God's plan to unfold. Your plan, or the *ego's plan*, on the other hand, will have you running around trying to make something happen. God's plan says to sit still and wait. If, and only if, you could understand this concept at the beginning of your transition, it would save you a great deal of pain, suffering, and regret. You must be singularly focused on one plan; you cannot implement your plan and God's plan simultaneously. It is one plan or the other, you choose.

Figure 6: Your Plan versus God's Plan

GOD'S PLAN	YOUR PLAN
-I know the plans for your life	-Created by the EGO
-Be still and Know I AM GOD	-I must do something
-Love-based	-Fear-based
-Response to TRUTH	-Response to a FALSE BELIEF

The Transition

The transition from working for a living to living for a living requires support, encouragement, inspiration and getting clear about who you are and how you want to powerfully show up in your life as yourself, as a businessperson, or as an entrepreneur. One of the first things on the list of must do's is to decide what *"showing up"* looks like. Now that you know who you are—the *image and likeness of God*, you get to decide how you show up to the world. In the business world, this is called branding. Branding is a tool that communicates to the world who you are and what you stand for. Let's explore this transition with a case example of Maya.

Get Clarity

Maya wanted clarity. The first thing she wanted to do was to clearly understand her purpose and define her intention.

> *"What is it I want to do?*
> *"Why do I want it?"*

"What does that look like?"

Maya realizes she has several spiritual gifts. She can see into the spirit realm. With years of transferable corporate skills, she wanted to learn how to integrate those skills into her spiritual practice. She sees herself as the *"Harriet Tubman"* of corporate America. She wants to help other women transition from the trap of labor to the freedom of service. Why? Because Maya wished someone had reached in and snatched her out of the hell she was in before she got fired. She wished there was someone who had successfully transitioned from a corporate J.O.B to living a more authentic lifestyle aligned with a divine purpose to show her the way. Because she did not have such a person in her life, Maya wanted to be a *way-shower* for women like herself who wanted to exit the corporate matrix and also wanted to know they would be financially ok. She was clear she intended to share everything she identified with the women she seeks to serve. Despite this clear intention, Maya did not know how to engage her ideal audience.

How would she find them?
How would they find her?

Most importantly, Maya wanted to know how to monetize her God-given gifts and talents so she could earn a living providing service to others. Maya had to brand herself. She wanted to stand out among other women doing similar work. She wanted to communicate who she was without appearing *cliché-ish*. She felt she had something unique to offer.

What is Branding?

Branding is not new. In the corporate world, branding encompasses everything, including the colors representing the brand on print and electronic materials, the logo, the motto, etc. It is all aspects of the company's presence to the public. You are your unique brand. Your brand is attractive to your clients. It is the way they see themselves in you. A brand is developed over time and may go through growing pains and changes. There is no reason to believe that once you have established a brand, you cannot expand it. You can. This is why McDonald grew their menu from burgers, fries, and shakes to everything we have today--chicken nuggets, salads, and gourmet coffee drinks. For the spiritual entrepreneur, your brand may change in many ways as you grow and acquire additional spiritual skills and gifts. The primary goal of branding is to ensure your audience can identify who you are and what you are doing to decide whether you are the right brand for their particular spiritual growth and developmental needs.

Why Brand?

Know, Like, and Trust. These are the key reasons why every social or spiritual entrepreneur must brand him or herself. You have the benefit of social media to assist with the *know* component. Social media gives you several platforms for your audience to get to know you. Social media will also provide you with feedback with *likes*. It will let you know if you are reaching your target audience and whether they like you or not. *Like* means they can stand behind you and what you stand for. *Trust* is where the *rubber meets the road.* Your potential clients must trust you enough to financially support you. You must provide your clients with a compelling reason, based on trust, to transfer money from their wallet to your wallet for providing a good or service. People will do business only with those they know, like, and trust. When all three components are in place, your clients will beat a path to your door for whatever you are providing.

Branding helps you to stand out in a crowd. My son loves pizza. He will eat pizza for breakfast, lunch, and dinner if he could. One day, when he was two years old, I recalled pulling up to a particular pizza chain that advertised $5 pizza, knowing full and well the child only eats a specific brand. I got a lesson in branding from a two-year-old regarding why he prefers one brand of pizza over the other.

We love brands! We live in them, drive them, eat them, educate them, buy them, and, most of all, promote our favorite brands. We notice brand names. We are programmed, through advertising, to believe one brand name is superior or more valuable than the generic. This is good news for spiritual entrepreneurs who naturally bring their uniqueness to the market. Spiritual seekers are usually looking for something specific. They may not know precisely what it is, but they know it right away when they see it. This is why you must, must brand.

Attraction Marketing

Branding entails knowing who you are, what your product is, and who your product is for. In the corporate world, advertising and marketing are used for this purpose. These agencies invest enormous amounts of money to position a product in the market for consumption. They are careful to consult psychologists and social scientists who profile markets based on what they believe motivates consumers to consume. In the spiritual community, attraction marketing, otherwise known as *"tribal branding,"* is a crucial strategy for branding (Hanlon, 2011). The purpose of tribal branding is to build a tribe of loyal followers who know, like, and trust you enough to consume your services, sing your praises, and promote your brand for you. Unlike traditional branding, primal branding is about building a community of like-minded individuals who believe in you and financially support your work.

Your vibe attracts your tribe.

Your Vibe

Your vibe attracts your tribe is the mantra of attraction marketing. You, your message, your uniqueness attracts your tribe. When they hear your message, they will know it is for them. Your responsibility is to keep being you. Authenticity sells! You do not have to go out and fan the flames of who you are. They have been waiting for you. Your tribe knows who you are, and they are waiting for you to show up consistently in their lives. These were Maya's concerns.

How do I develop a tribe?
How will my tribe find me?
How will I show up for my tribe?

Your tribe is out there. They are already looking for you. They will find you. But how? You show up! You tell the world who you are and why they should follow you. Your tribe will find you through attraction marketing. You simply have to become attractive to your audience by being exactly who you are.

Primal Branding

According to Hanlon (2011), primal branding entails building a community of people who share your belief system. He presents seven components of primal branding that are necessary to create a brand and a belief system to attract only those who you want to be drawn to you. He notes incorporating all seven components is essential to attract and retain your tribe. In the case of light-workers and the spiritual community, primal branding begins with a powerful intention. Spiritual intentions must be written clearly and communicated through your brand. Below is an example of an intention written by my coach. Pay particular attention to the language and word choice. Every word has an, a vibration. Every word matters.

Intention

To magnetize a large, ever-expanding, loyal tribe who loves me, my message and the work I do; who trust me because I am deeply trustworthy; who readily, happily and repeatedly buys from me and refers others to buy from me as well. I accomplished this by adding immense VALUE to as many lives as I can.
And so it is!

Take a moment to let this intention sink in. What jumped out at you? What got your attention? How do you see the principles of tribal branding incorporated in this intention statement? Let's explore.

Components of Tribal Branding

Once you learn these seven components or *"emotional touchpoints,"* you will be able to craft a powerful intention that will attract a tribe of amazing souls who believe in you, are deeply passionate about your work, loves your authenticity and financially supports your work. We begin with the *Creation Story*.

The Creation Story

Your creation story is how you introduce yourself to your tribe. Who are you and where did you come from? Why are you the one? The purpose of your creation story is to communicate this information.

My creation story begins with a little girl growing up in abject poverty in a muddy little village in a developing nation; abandoned as a child to live with her grandmother who healed her with plant and bush medicine. She immigrated to the United States to live with her abusive parents. She excelled academically studying sociology of health and medicine and became a college professor of social work. Disillusioned with her chosen career, she left academia to reclaim her spiritual gifting and identity as a powerful plant healer. This is my creation story in a nutshell!

The Creed

Every spiritual brand ideally should have a clearly articulated "creed" or your *modus operandi*. You have to communicate to the world the words you live by thus attracting those on your level. For me, my brand entails international travel to geo-spiritual places around the globe. If you are afraid to fly, this is not the brand for you. My brand honors freedom above all. Bondage to a job or circumstance is seen as a wrong choice. If this does not resonate with you, again, this may not be the brand for you. Your creed communicates who you are and weeds out those not aligned with you or the belief system shared by your tribe. Branding is a great sifter.

The Icons

Similar to logos, icons are powerful symbols representing your brand. More than a logo, an icon is something so universal that when anyone sees it, automatically, it evokes deep sub-conscious emotion. For example, when Christians see a crucifix or cross, they immediately have an emotional response. The cross is a symbol of peace, but it has been used to rally men to war. Similarly, your icon should emote passion and identification with your tribe.

The Rituals

All tribes have rituals. Brand rituals have nothing to do with the occult. They are intended to create brand cohesiveness among the tribe. You must identify the rituals associated with your brand. Where do these come from? They come from you! You create them. What do you do daily that you can share with your tribe? What rituals can you create for your tribe? I grew up watching Amateur Night at the Apollo. One ritual all contestants performed was rubbing a large tree stump for good luck as they entered the stage. I do not know of one person in the history of the Apollo who has not rubbed that tree stump for good luck. You can create new rituals at any time. You can go live on social media at the same time each day. This gives your tribe a ritual to know where you are and where to find you. I remember when the television show <u>Miami Vice</u> aired primetime on Friday. No one I knew went out until AFTER the show was over. When I was in college, students would change their class schedule just to catch Oprah on daytime TV! This was serious tribal behavior. The most important thing for you to know is that your tribe organizes around the ritual you create. Create rituals for your tribe.

Non-believers

Non-believers are a blessing! They are who your tribe is not. These are the people who will never support you or your work. Non-believers are your biggest critics and greatest gift. Though it may seem like they are out to get you, they are the ones who will keep you relevant and on your toes without having to pay them a dime in consulting cost. I think that is a great deal! Knowing who you are *NOT*, is just as important as knowing who you are.

Sacred Words

Sacred words are words that resonate with you and your tribe. When your tribe hears these words, they know you are talking to them. Sacred words are powerful, emotional and spiritual connectors because they let you know you belong to the tribe. If you are to be a member of the tribe, you must know the lingo and use it accordingly. Every time I encounter my spiritual life coach, she always asks me, *"How you lovin?"* My response is always, *"I'm loving gooooood!"* As a member of her tribe, I expect this greeting each and every time we connect. I could just imagine how crushed I would feel if she did not address me with the same beautiful question every time.

The Leader

Every tribe has a leader. In this case, the leader is you. Who you are is critically important to your tribe. You are the visionary of your vision, the leader of the tribe. My coach calls herself our *"Sherpa."* She is a leader who walks the walk first and then guides us along the path. Your tribe will trust you because you did the work on your spiritual path. You took all the bumps and bruises and now you have the wisdom to impart to your tribe. It takes time to become a leader. It takes time to develop the intestinal fortitude to stand in the fire, (sometimes alone), and suffer public ridicule, setbacks, and failures. A leader bounces back quickly from negativity with a renewed strength and belief in self. Leaders do not see failure they see lessons learned. Your tribe will trust you because of who you are and what you have endured on your spiritual walk. They want your expertise so they can avoid the pain of the pits and accelerate learning.

Maya's Journey

Maya's transition from working for a living to living for a living was a success. She has a thriving motivational speaking practice where she reaches women in corporate America. Maya's underlying message in her motivational speeches is to remind these powerful women to remember the dreams they had before life became so complicated. She asks them to consider the idea that reconnecting to those dreams might be the path to wild, unbelievable success. Maya has taken care to incorporate the principles of primal branding to create a brand that achieves this goal. She knows her spiritual message has to be buried amongst the motivational content. She also knows her tribe will feel her vibe. In a room full of women, she expects only a few will get what she is all about. She expects those women who truly hear her message will be the ones who will join her tribe.

I must have decided wrongly if I am not at peace. ACIM

22 CHAPTER 22

CONCLUSION

Experiencing peace in your life is the signal that you have chosen correctly. If you are not at peace at your job or if your appointment is not serving you, if you cannot quit because you need the money, you have chosen wrongly. O.M.G.! What are you saying, Dr. Bacchus? Are you saying all the sleepless nights studying in college to be qualified for the job I have now was wrong? Are you saying the career I worked so hard to develop was the wrong choice? Do you realize I was the first in my family to go to college? I graduated and inspired my baby cousins to go to college too. Was that a wrong choice?? I am the one who holds my family together financially. If it were not for me, I do not know where we would be. I am the one who is responsible for making sure the family operates like a well-oiled machine. I did all of this with hard work and determination. Was all of that a wrong choice too?

No, dear. I am saying that *if* you are at a job or have a career or whatever you want to call it AND you are unhappy, OR the job is making you sick, OR you cannot wait to retire, OR you hate going to work, OR you are being bullied, OR you have not had a raise in years, OR no promotion yet, etc.; you have made a wrong choice. If what you are doing with your career is not bringing you bliss, peace, and joy, it is the wrong choice. Ok, I know these statements are fully loaded; however, look around, do you see peace at your job? Do you fit in? Do you even like going there? If it were not for the paycheck, would you go? Do you believe the only way you can earn a living is with a J.O.B.? If this is so, this is wrong thinking.

Think about it, why would any intelligent human being with full knowledge of *Self* deliberately choose to work in a stress-provoking environment for 30-40 years of their prime adult lives? What part of your mind thinks it is ok to suffer for one second to earn a living? What part of your mind allows suffering to become the out-picturing of your life experiences? Well, the part of your mind that is sick. Only a sick mind allows you to choose pain when pleasure is equally available.

Workplace Voodoo gives you the option of healing your mind and heart so you will naturally choose peace instead of pain. It allows you to see the fullness of who you are and the value of your natural God-given talents and gifts. Workplace Voodoo creates the mental space for you to believe you can share your gifts with the world and be highly compensated.

At a basic level, Workplace Voodoo is the process of coming into the awareness that your job is providing the context or the *path of least resistance* nudging you to raise your level of consciousness from *Victim* to *Manifester* and beyond. Jobs provide the necessary contrast for you to know what you want in your life by experiencing what you do not wish to. I am sure you can clearly articulate what your dream life would look like *if* you had no stress. What would your life look like if you had all the money and social support you require?

What if you had no worries, and no one was out to get you? What would this life look like to you? This life would be very peaceful, right? But most of you do not have this lifestyle. Why? Choices! At the exact moment, you identify what you do not want, the polar opposite is instantly created in the spiritual realm. Your soul, the eternal part of you, aligns with this desire and sets out to deliver this life to you. So why do you not have your big, fat, juicy peach of a life? One reason is that although your soul knows the way, your ego is still running the show. You are listening to your ego and making decisions out of fear of the future—most of it based on lack and limitation around money.

Will I have enough money to retire?
Will I have enough money for the children's college?
How long will I be able to afford my lifestyle into old age?

In my case, my ego was a persona named Denise N. A. Bacchus, a character in the drama on the stage of my life running my show. Her attachment to *her 0-7 what had happened story* set her out on a path that guaranteed her great worldly success on one side of the pole and deep pain and suffering on the other side of the pole.

She entered the rat race the same way she entered each phase of my life—she did what "*they*" told her what to do. And she complied out of fear of reprisal. *They* said to go to college and get a job. She did. *They* said to get a tenure-track position. She did. Because there were no mistakes, she was led to a place where the job was supposed to be her dream job. The mark of all her success turned into a living nightmare. The job that was supposed to provide for her and take care of her needs was hurting her and causing her physical pain? How?

The Ego Illusion

Despite all the symptoms of stress, I felt I was progressing nicely along my life path. Like Michelle Obama, I was checking off boxes. I was excelling in teaching, research, and service to the academic community. I was well trained and felt confident in my duties. Yet the intense workday as junior faculty required me to bring my work home to keep up. I was extremely exhausted, and I was stressing out my family too. I kept going. The illusion of the ego was convincing my mind that my body could do anything, even if it was utterly falling apart right before me. By the end of my first academic year, I was checking off other boxes too, but at my doctor's office—high blood pressure, thyroid disorder, stress, and anxiety on my intake forms. I knew this vicious cycle had to be interrupted. *But how?* Quit my job? Get a divorce? Send the kids to boarding school???

Choices

Given I had written an entire dissertation on stress and coping among professional Black women, I had the answer. It was right in my face—use my spirituality is a resource for coping with the stress. I could not see it. My ego kept me in the illusion of working hard no matter the cost, but my soul also has chosen bliss. The work-related stress I was experiencing occurred to draw my attention to the notion that perhaps I was on the wrong path. All along, the stress was gently asking me to consider another route. Each time I left a job, I got another one—different place, same drama.

When I continued to choose jobs over my divine purpose, getting fired was precisely what needed to happen to catapult me onto my spiritual journey. My soul, the eternal me, the part of me that is real, knows the divine blueprint for my life. It recognizes the next steps.

How does the soul know the plan?

Because my soul was with God when the plan was hatched. Your soul has been speaking to you all your life. It tells you what brings you pain and what brings you pleasure. Heck, God has been speaking to you too. Even the angels and your ancestors have been communicating with you. They sent you all kinds of signs, and they continue to address them. You ignored them all. The church told you to pray harder. Believe more. You did. You felt better, but no sustained change. Your ego says, rely on yourself—you are in control; you have to figure everything out. Your ego says keep grinding in the rat race, you will succeed. The ego says to play it safe. Stay in your comfort zone. Everything will be just fine, right? Wrong!

God will never tell you to stay in your comfort zone. There is no growth in the comfort zone. Growth is uncomfortable and inevitable. God said, let us co-create, and I will show you the plans I have for you. God is about expansion and new experiences. Stress on the spiritual level is your soul's navigation system alerting you that you are waaaaaay off course of the God plan for your life. Your soul's navigation system is gently repeating,

Proceed to the route, Proceed to the route.

Your ego is saying,

Go this way, it's easier, and there's more money.

What about free will? Yes, you have the right to self-determination. This is your God-given birthright. We all have the right to create anything we want to create while we are here. And we do. Some people create good stuff, and others create some real f**ced up shit! I know I did. Without spiritual grounding and guidance, you are prone to create a big mess of everything. By the time I encounter women like you, they have been stressed out for a long, long time. Workplace Voodoo interrupts the hamster wheel mentality enslaving human beings in a job. It is coming into the awareness that jobs cause job stress. No job, no job stress.

> *But where will I live?*
> *How will I eat?*
> *Who is going to pay all these bills?*

Matthew 6:25 instructs you not to worry about these things. It reminds you that your source is God, and God will provide ALL your needs. But you must shift your egoic mind from lack and limitation to that of abundance. You must have FAITH!

Price's (1994) abundance wealth training teaches you how to coming into full awareness of God's abundance, your true nature when you *overstand* this abundance statement:

Money is not my supply. No person, place, or condition is my supply. My awareness, understanding, and knowledge of the all-providing activity of the Divine Mind within me IS my supply. My consciousness of this Truth is unlimited. Therefore my supply is unlimited.

Use the chapters in Workplace Voodoo to build your faith to shift your consciousness to the Divine Mind of abundance. There are many paths to raising your consciousness. There are no wrong choices. Even if you believe you made a wrong choice, there is always a consolation prize, there is always a ram in the bush, there is still a new learning or wisdom for you to obtain. Workplace Voodoo helps you focus on yourself and what you have to do to finally end the needless suffering and live your authentic divine life as the image and likeness of God. You are creators. You are here to use your divine power to co-create your big, fat, juicy peach of life with your Soul in the driver's seat and full trust in God. It is your responsibility to raise your level of consciousness to the understanding that whether you believe in this voodoo or not, you are on a spiritual journey involving the job you have now. This is where the awakening begins.

Workplace Voodoo brings you into the *overstanding* that this book did not accidentally land in your hands. I wrote this book for you. This is why you are reading it now. Buckle up and enjoy the ride. So far, with all your intelligence, you have been choosing what you do not want. Imagine what your life would look like when you deliberately create the life that you do want. It may look like Marion Parke, a podiatric surgeon who daydreamed about developing her line of shoes while completing her residency in podiatry. One day, she answered her heart's desire. She decided to put down her scalpel and pick up her sketchbook to design a collection of shoes that are luxurious as well as anatomically perfect for women's feet. How about David Otunga? He is a Harvard educated lawyer who abandoned his practice to become a reality show actor and later a World Wrestling Entertainment wrestler? There are so many examples of people who transformed their lives from what they thought they were supposed to be *doing* to *being* exactly who they were created to be. What will be your story? Use the spiritual resources for coping in this book. Do the work. Test it out for yourself. Again if you are not experiencing peace, you have chosen wrongly. You can choose peace instead. The way to end work-related stress is <u>Workplace Voodoo</u>.

⌘

ABOUT THE AUTHOR

Dr. Bacchus is an accomplished academic professor and quantitative researcher. Her focus is on applying theory to reduce work-related stress and increase positive coping outcomes. She authored one of the only books on stress and coping among professional Black women. At the height of her career, Dr. Bacchus answered the call of her soul and left the classroom to reclaim her identity as a powerful spiritual healer. She travels the world to expand her knowledge of spiritual healing practices and plant medicine. Dr. Bacchus lives part-time in the United States, Guyana, South American, and Eleuthera, Bahamas, where she considers staring at crystal blue water essential to her spiritual practice. She hosts the most amazing retreats in geo-spiritual locations around the globe. She also travels the world with her children, Philana and Andrés.

REFERENCES

Bacchus, D.N.A. (2008). Coping with work-related stress: A study of the use of coping resources among professional black women. *Journal of Ethnic and Cultural Diversity in Social Work.* 17(1) 60-81.

Bacchus, D.N.A., Holly, L. (2005). Spirituality as a coping response: The experiences of professional Black women. *Journal of Ethnic and Cultural Diversity in Social Work.* 13(4) 65-84.

Bacchus, D. N. A. (2008). Stress and coping among professional Black women: An application of coping theory and use of coping resources. VDM Verlag Dr. Mueller E.K.: Germany

Beckwith, M. B. (2013). Life visioning: A transformative process for activating your unique gifts and highest potential. Sounds True: CA.

Bell, A., Rajenan, D., & Theiler, S. (2012). Spirituality at work: an employee stress intervention for academics? *International Journal of Business and Social Science*, 3(11).

Dorfman, R. A. (2015). Paradigms of clinical social work. Routledge.

Folkman, S., Lazarus, R. S., Gruen, R. J., & DeLongis, A. (1986). Appraisal, coping, health status, and psychological symptoms. *Journal of personality and social psychology*, 50(3), 571.

Foundation for Inner Peace. (1976). A course in miracles. Foundation for Inner peace: CA.

Halon, P. (2011). Primal branding: Create zealots for your brand, your company, and your future.

Hinrichs, J., DeFife, J., & Westen, D. (2011). Personality subtypes in adolescent and adult children of alcoholics: a two-part study. *The Journal of nervous and mental disease*, *199*(7), 487.

Kouffman Sherman, P. (2016). The book of sacred baths: 52 bathing rituals to revitalize your spirit. Llewellyn Publications: Woodbury, MN.

Love, V. (2017). 40 Mantras-40 Days to wealth consciousness book and journal. Butterfly Rising Production.

Love, V. (2018). 40 Spells-40 days to wealth consciousness book and journal. Butterfly Rising Production.

Love, V. (2018). 40 scriptures-bibliomancy for enlightenment wealth book and journal. Butterfly Rising Production.

Lea, J. (2018) Core perfectum: What you don't know about your heart may be killing your life.

McLeod, S. (2007). Maslow's hierarchy of needs. Simply psychology, 1.

Michaele, M. & Portfield, C. (2014). Hoodoo bible magic: Sacred secrets of scriptures sorcery. Missionary Independent Spiritual Church.

Miller, J. (2012). Financial sorcery: Magical strategies to create real and lasting wealth. New Page Books: Pompton Plains: NJ.

Myss, C. (2002). Sacred contracts: Awakening your divine potential. Bantam Books.

Neff, A. (2018). Llewellyn's witches' spell-a-day almanac: Holidays & love spells, rituals & meditations. Llewellyn's Worldwide, Ltd.

Oribello, W.A. (2007). Bible spells: obtain your every desire by activating the secret meaning of hundreds of biblical verses. Inner Light Publications: New Brunswick: NJ.

Pollard, S. (1963). Factory discipline in the industrial revolution. *Economic History Review*, 254-271.

Riva, A. (1982). Powers of the psalms. International Imports.

Sampson, R. J., & Wilson, W. J. (1995). Toward a theory of race, crime, and urban inequality. *Race, crime, and justice: A reader, 1995*, 37-56.

Tipping, C. (2009). Radical forgiveness. Sounds. True Inc.: Boulder, CO.

Thomas, A. J., Witherspoon, K. M., & Speight, S. L. (2004). Toward the development of the stereotypic roles for Black women scale. *Journal of Black Psychology, 30*(3), 426-442.

Widick, C., Parker, C. A., & Knefelkamp, L. (1978). Erik Erikson and psychosocial development. New directions for student services,1978(4),1-17.

Yronwode, C. & Strabo, M. (2013). The art of hoodoo candle magic in rootwork, conjure, and spiritual church services. Missionary Independent Spiritual Church.

Yronwode, C. (2013). The black folder: personal communications of the mastery of hoodoo. Missionary Independent Spiritual Church.

YouTube Videos

Beck with, M. B. (June 21, 2018) The 4 Stages Of spiritual awakening | Michael Bernard Beckwith. Mind Valley.

WEBSITES

Sigal, S. (November 5, 2018). The Witches of Baltimore: Young black women are leaving Christianity and embracing African witchcraft in digital covens (SIGAL SAMUEL).

Resources

Please go to **www.drdenisebacchus.com**
for more information on:

- Booking a Workplace Voodoo discovery session.

    o Cubical conjuring.
    o Spiritual decoding and alignment.
    o Plant medicinal assessments.
    o And much more…

- Purchasing natural botanical products for your home and personal use.

- Speaking engagements and tours.

- Upcoming luxury geo-spiritual retreats.

Workplace
Voodoo

Made in the USA
Las Vegas, NV
12 October 2021